P9-DIZ-861

America's Dilemma:
JOBS VS. PRICES

Also by Alfred L. Malabre, Jr.

UNDERSTANDING THE ECONOMY:
For People Who Can't Stand Economics

America's Dilemma:

JOBS VS. PRICES

by Alfred L. Malabre, Jr.

DODD, MEAD & COMPANY, NEW YORK

Printed in the United States of America

1 2 3 4 5 6 7 8 9 10

Library of Congress Cataloging in Publication Data

Malabre, Alfred L
America's dilemma.

Includes index.
1. Inflation (Finance) and unemployment—United States. I. Title.
HD5724.M233 330.9'73'092 78-18809
ISBN 0-396-07586-X

For Ann, John and Richard

Contents

America's Dilemma:
JOBS VS. PRICES

CHAPTER ONE

A Loss of Faith

When Jimmy Carter took the oath of Presidential office in January 1977, there was a sense of cautious relief across the 200-year-old nation. The previous decade-and-a-half had ben painful indeed for most Americans. A young, charismatic President had been assassinated, cut down in Dallas by a sniper. His successor, utterly devoid of charisma, built expectations of a "Great Society" but in the end produced only a society that grated, ridden by mounting economic distress at home and a wretched, unwinnable war in a faraway place.

There followed Mr. Nixon and his unholy entourage, led by the Haldeman-Ehrlichman combination. The Nixon years are now remembered mainly for the Watergate misdeeds, for still further ruinous conflict abroad, for a corrosive epidemic of inflation at home, for the onset of the longest, and in some ways the harshest, business recession suffered in America since the depression years before World War II.

The unelected, unsought presidency of Gerald Ford, brief and mercifully uneventful, brought the start of a healing, the tentative resumption of a trust between the country's leadership and its citizenry.

And so, when Jimmy Carter stood before Chief Justice Warren Burger at noon on the steps of the Capitol building in Washington on January 20, 1977, a cold, sparklingly clear day, there was a sense of cautious relief that perhaps the awful times were behind. When the new President, hatless and coatless in the crisp winter air, praised Mr. Ford for helping to heal the country's wounds, the ovation that ensued was long and loud, reflecting a widespread recognition that, yes, things at long last were on the mend in America. No one supposed, to be sure, that the millennium had finally arrived. But the mood, for the first time in a long time, was timidly optimistic. The reasoned judgment of a large cross-section of thoughtful Americans was that the nation could at last begin to move ahead again, albeit more gingerly than in past decades, hopefully more wisely. The awful succession of crises, extending from a Dallas street to Vietnam to the Watergate apartment complex in Washington, appeared largely resolved.

The horizon in early 1977 still contained clouds. The Russian military menace remained. The messy Mideast, with its combustible ingredients of Arab-Israeli hostility and a painfully politicized petroleum supply, was still there. Distressing poverty continued across much of the massive population of the unindustrialized Third World, in countries as far away as India and as near as sunny Jamaica, just beneath Florida's toe.

But these were familiar problems, whose persistence could hardly be blamed on simply the continued blundering of American policymakers. At last, it seemed to many Americans when Jimmy Carter took that oath administered by Warren Burger, the blundering—the mistakes that could have been avoided with more than a modicum of governmental wisdom—was largely over.

Most unfortunately, this was not the case. A monumental blunder—avoidable, potentially disastrous for the nation—remained in early 1977 very much in progress.

The purpose of this book is to explore America's overriding dilemma as the nation faces the final two decades of this century. Gunnar Myrdal, Nobel-laureate economist from Sweden, once wrote a book titled *An American Dilemma.* The dilemma that Mr. Myrdal discussed was the dilemma presented by the plight of the American black man and black woman. In 1977 that great problem assuredly had not evaporated in the United States. But the situation of the American black, the relationship between the country's major races, was vastly sounder than back in the 1940's, when Mr. Myrdal's study appeared. That is not the dilemma to be explored in this book.

* * *

A dilemma, Mr. Webster tells us, is a problem seemingly incapable of a satisfactory solution. The key word in that definition is "*seemingly.*" A dilemma, we submit, isn't worth exploring in the first place unless it can be resolved. What is the purpose of dwelling extensively on hopeless matters? Surely, there is enough gloom and doom about us. We do not need to seek more out unnecessarily. But there is a need to speak out clearly when a danger is as obvious as it is now and a solution is possible.

The great dilemma confronting the American nation today is deeply social, in that it involves the very roots of a unique freedom. The dilemma is also intensely economic. Widely recognized, and widely viewed as hopelessly intractable, it is the dilemma of prices and jobs, inflation and unemployment. It is the idea that America's fabled economy, farm and factory *nonpareil,* can no longer function without one or the other evil—high joblessness or spiraling prices—and increasingly must function with more than a taste of both.

This book will explore that dilemma, attempt to demonstrate how dangerous and how needless it is, and, in the process, spell out ways in which it can be resolved. The stake, almost unrecognized in the general relief after more than a decade of national troubles, is huge. For if the dilemma is accepted—the idea that the country's economy can no longer function without either painful unemployment or painful inflation—then our long-standing system will inevitably be changed in unwelcome ways. And we will have lost, no doubt irretrievably, an economic arrangement—based upon incentive and individual initiative—that has proved to be the most productive and broadly beneficial in human history. To avoid such an unfortunate unfolding of events, American leaders now must move with exceptional wisdom. They must see that the dilemma of inflation and unemployment need not be.

In summary, then, we submit that the traditional American economic system is in danger. It is endangered by the dilemma to be explored in this book. At stake, ultimately, is the fundamental nature of the nation's economy.

What is that nature?

It can be glimpsed, among other places, in the writing of Adam Smith, in *The Wealth of Nations,* his masterpiece, published by strange coincidence in 1776, the year of America's birth. "It is not from the benevolence of the butcher, the brewer, or the baker that we expect our dinner," he wrote, "but from their regard for their self-interest."

Adam Smith had further observations that pertain to the nature of our economic system today. "Every individual," he maintained, "endeavors to employ his capital so that its produce may be of greatest value; he generally neither intends to promote the public interest, nor knows how much he is promoting it; he intends only his own security, only his own gain; and he is led by an invisible hand to promote an end which was no part of his own intention; by pursuing his own interest he frequently promotes that of society more efficiently than when he really intends to promote it."

Initiative, Mr. Webster says, is energy or aptitude displayed in action. In the ideal world of the egalitarian, the butcher, the brewer and the baker are altruistic to the extent that our dinner would materialize as a result of their interest in us, their concern for us, not from any self-interest. In such a world, initiative derives from altruism, and energy and aptitude flourish without need of guidance by an "invisible hand."

* * *

Arthur Okun, a prominent economics professor who served as chief economic adviser to the late President Lyndon Johnson, reflects an influential point-of-view—the idea that an egalitarian American system is not only desirable but practical. He maintains that to "give every citizen an equal share of the national income would give added recognition to the moral worth of every citizen, to the mutual respect of citizens for one another, and to equivalent value of membership in a society for all."

There is no mention of initiative or self-interest, only of the virtues of equality. And, it should be stressed, the sentiment comes not from a flower-child or poet or minister of the church, but a man recently near the center of national power, nowadays an adviser to powerful business corporations, highly respected at Yale University where he has taught and where academic training is provided for many of tomorrow's national leaders.

It is occasionally argued that the nation, after all its recent troubles, has grown more practical, more cognizant of its economic and political limitations. Perhaps that may eventually prove to be the case. But for now, the prevailing national attitude can best be summed up by recalling a remark of Norman B. Ture, a Washington-based economic consultant whose expertise centers in matters of taxation and wealth distribution. "We are in an era in which egalitarians are in full cry, rather than in disorderly retreat as they are sometimes pictured," Mr. Ture observed.

* * *

The nature of America's economy is simple enough. To function smoothly, there must be initiative, personal and corporate. In recent years, as inflation has grown increasingly intractable, as unemployment has become stickier in good times and ever more distressing in bad times, there has developed a sense that the economy is somehow deeply flawed, that it no longer works, that we must search for a new arrangement.

This loss of faith, which lamentably cuts across the country's political spectrum and embraces an exceedingly wide assortment of citizens, can be readily documented.

Who could be more pro-American than Lawrence Welk,

the bandleader from Yankton, South Dakota? Mr. Welk would be the first to concede that he is no economist. But he does reflect the views, we suspect, of a broad segment of the American citizenry, people who may not possess postgraduate degrees in business administration from, say, Harvard University. But people who have a lot of commonsense, who have managed to fare reasonably well under the rules of the country's economic system.

The weekly magazine, *U.S. News & World Report*, recently interviewed this ebullient, successful bandleader, asking him about America's prospects in general, including its economic prospects.

"We are still operating under the free-enterprise system," Mr. Welk declared. However, he added, "it is not as effective as it used to be, and that is too bad because it helped to provide the vitality which made this country strong."

Mr. Welk had more to say: "If we don't change before long, we're going to have a country controlled from Washington, D.C. There will be more people on the public payroll operating out of Washington than are really working and paying taxes out here in the rest of the country." He concluded: "The biggest danger in this trend is that we will end up surrendering a lot of our freedoms to the bureaucrats."

The Gallup poll recently conducted an interesting survey. The polling organization sampled more than 9,000 people, not only in the U.S. but abroad. One of the questions sought to determine: "What are your fears and worries for the future?" Worry over health was number one in most countries but in the U.S. the number two concern, running a very close race with worry over health, was worry over "economic instability." The Gallup poll showed that 21 percent of Americans regarded the economy as their number one worry, a bigger worry than health. Only seven percent of West Europeans viewed economic worries as foremost. Other percentages, with regard to economic worries, ranged from as high as 10 percent among person in the Far East to only one percent among Africans.

Clearly, Americans are deeply disturbed about their country's economy. Not so many years ago the U.S. economy was widely viewed as wonderfully sound and certainly not a reason for major concern.

Tilford Gaines, senior vice president and chief economist of Manufacturers Hanover Trust of New York, is among those now concerned. "There has never in recent memory been a shortage of economic doomsayers," the economist declares. Perhaps, he goes on, "our type of capitalist system is fundamentally unstable, and must eventually lead to a greater concentration of authority in the government in order to protect the well-being of all the citizens of the community."

The erosion of faith in the U.S. economic system, as it has evolved over many prosperous decades since the Great Depression of the 1930's, can be detected similarly in the remarks of leaders of highly successful labor organizations, powerful enterprises whose members have fared better than many Americans.

Hark, for instance, to George Meany, president of the AFL-CIO: "It is no exaggeration to say that the idea of a free, democratic, enlightened society is in jeopardy" in the United States.

Arthur F. Burns, a top economic adviser to four American presidents and chairman for many years of the Federal Reserve Board, hardly qualifies as a disciple of George Meany or of any other U.S. labor leader. The economist will be remembered, most assuredly, as a somewhat professorial pipe-puffing, rather conservative, rather pro-business gentleman. Yet, Mr. Burns repeatedly has warned that the U.S. economic system is in trouble, that, as he once put it, the old, time-tested laws of our free-enterprise economy don't seem to work properly any longer.

"Our country is engaged in a fateful debate," Mr. Burns has stated, adding somewhat ominously that "America has become enmeshed in an inflationary web, and we need—all of us—to gather our moral strength to extricate ourselves."

* * *

Underlying the pessimism of such economists as Arthur Burns and Tilford Gaines, of such labor leaders as George Meany, of so many Americans including Lawrence Welk, is a phenomenon that can be described in many ways. In the highly esoteric language of economists, for example, the phenomenon can be described as a "rightward shift of the Phillips curve."

That isn't as forbidding as it may sound. The so-called Phillips curve was conceived by a British economist named A. W. Phillips. It is, quite simply, a curve on which are plotted on the left, vertically, rates of inflation and at the bottom, horizontally, extending to the right, unemployment rates. The curve itself is merely a reflection of the amount of inflation recorded when unemployment happens to be at a particular level. Professor Phillips observed that low rates of unemployment generally combine with high rates of inflation, and vice versa. In the late 1950's, for example, the Phillips curve showed that an unemployment rate of about five and one-half percent was accompanied by an annual inflation rate of about one percent. In 1957, when the balance between the twin economic evils of inflation and unemployment was somewhat more evenly distributed, an unemployment rate just over four percent coexisted with an inflation rate of just over three percent.

The curve that Professor Phillips charted in those relatively early post-World War II years formed a neat crescent that swung gently from the upper left area of the page, in concave fashion, out toward the lower right area of the page. The message contained in the crescent was clear: low rates of unemployment tend to coincide with high rates of inflation and high unemployment rates tend to accompany low inflation rates. The optimum situation, it appeared from the Phillips curve, was a compromise, roughly in the crescent's middle, where there were no extremes. This optimum situation, in the 1950's and into the 1960's, seemed to occur where unemployment held at roughly four percent and inflation perhaps one notch lower. In this regard, the aforementioned 1957 record was reasonably close to ideal.

The "rightward shift" of the Phillips curve is a reasonably recent development. What has happened, in brief, is that the British professor's little crescent has moved to the right of the page, and in the process also floated upward slightly. As a result, the middle of the crescent that traces the unemployment-inflation relationship during recent years reflects very different statistics than those prevailing, say, in 1957. The midsection of a Phillips curve covering recent years reflects an unemployment rate of close to six percent and an inflation rate of roughly five percent. By comparison, six percent unemployment on a Phillips curve drawn during the 1950's coincides with an inflation rate of about one percent.

The rightward shift of the Phillips curve in recent years—and there can be no doubt that such a shift is evident—is deeply distressing to students of the American economy. In effect, the shift indicates that the economy is growing more prone to both inflation and unemployment. Years ago, it was generally believed that inflation and unemployment were, in effect, the opposite ends of an economic seesaw. A study of the Phillips curve by New York's Citibank observed that "as one goes up, the other goes down, in a relatively predictable proportion."

As long as the seesaw could be balanced readily, with neither end too far above the ground, the consensus view was that the country's free-enterprise system could operate in fairly satisfactory fashion. Sellers of goods and services could remain free for the most part to decide with their customers what prices would be paid. Workers could remain free for the most part to decide with their employers what wage levels would prevail.

The rightward shift of the Phillips curve has cast deep doubt across such assumptions. The shift seems to suggest, to many observers, that the economy has grown too inflation-prone, too unemployment-prone. Inflation remains high even when unemployment is high. And, when unemployment begins to approach levels once deemed barely tolerable, inflation starts soaring. The economy's flexibility, it would appear, has diminished greatly. The reasonable balance of the old seesaw is gone. Whenever the seesaw begins to approach a reasonable balance today, the ground is dangerously far below. Our feet dangle without support.

The rightward shift of the Phillips curve is merely one means used by many economists to describe what seems so distressing about today's economic picture.

* * *

Especially disturbing are the implications of the shift. If the economy no longer operates so that comfortably low joblessness and comfortably low inflation can coexist, then a fundamental premise of the country's traditional free-enterprise arrangement is invalidated—the free working of the economic marketplace, between buyer and seller, between worker and employer, ceases to operate in a tolerable manner. The end of this gloomy road, the scenario that begins to emerge, seems to many observers to be an economy that must increasingly be regulated. They reason that if marketplace forces can only operate alongside intolerable inflation and intolerable unemployment, then greater regulation must be imposed on the marketplace.

In the process, of course, freedom in the country must erode. Wages must be set. Prices must be set.

The question of whether freedom must erode in the process brings to mind a comment, made in the eighteenth century, by Alexander Fraser Tytler, an eminent Scottish historian. "A democracy," he warned, "could not exist as a permanent form of government. It can only exist until the majority of voters discovers that they can vote themselves largess out of the public treasury. From that moment on, the majority always votes for the candidate who promises them the most benefits from the public treasury, with the result that democracy always collapses." The Scot added, ominously, that this collapse was "always to be followed by a dictatorship."

Along a similar vein, Robert L. Heilbroner, the American economic historian, stresses what a unique adventure the American free-enterprise experience is. Free-enterprise capitalism, he once observed, is an economic arrangement that "most of mankind has never had, does not now have, and in all probability will never have any contact with." A loss of freedom, he added, "is hardly a loss to men who have never known liberty." He is among many respected analysts who appear convinced that the country's economic system, already a stranger to "most of mankind," is destined to disappear, to be replaced presumably by a collectivism in which, to borrow from the economists' jargon once again, there will be no rightward movement of any Phillips curve.

* * *

The pity, and the impetus for this book, is that Americans have known liberty, do know liberty, and, we submit, have within themselves, within the country's varied resources, the ability to improve the system, to make it work better, to give the lie to arguments holding that there is an inevitability about our increasing proneness toward inflation and joblessness.

The quick, superficial response to the economic problem is, of course, stricter, broader regulation of economic matters by the governmental bureaucracy. The danger, just as obviously, is spelled out by Samuel P. Huntington, a professor of government at Harvard. "Bureaucrats," he cautions, "will exploit democratic processes for their own purposes, making it impossible for other groups to compete effectively with them." The warning of Alexander Tytler is recalled.

Max Beloff, a professor of government and public administration at Britain's Oxford University, ponders the question of free enterprise's future in America. He shares the view that it is in jeopardy, in large part on account of the distressing economic record of recent years. However, his conclusions are not without a modicum of hope. "I'm not at all sure that democracy can work," he states. But then he goes on to add that such systems do have a chance "under the very exceptional circumstances existing in the U.S." Free enterprise has worked in America—and keeps doing so—because, he explains, "of the great degree of decentralization imposed by the size of the country; where democracy seems to break down is in highly centralized countries where there are no built-in checks to what a temporary majority can do—like Britain."

A glimmer of optimism can also be detected in the comments of Friedrich A. Hayek, who has taught at such institutions as the University of Salzburg, the University of Chicago and London University, and is among the very few economists, along with Gunnar Myrdal, to be awarded a Nobel Prize. "It would be wrong to say that democracy has failed and therefore is doomed," he says. "Nobody can seriously doubt the efficiency of the private-enterprise system and its superiority, but many people resent the fact that it distributes wealth according to market values, rather than needs."

The economics professor is quick to concede that the virtues of free enterprise are often obscured by the well-publicized problems of inflation and unemployment. But he firmly believes that "I don't think we ought to say that democracy has failed." Indeed, when he compares American free enterprise with the "dictatorships" prevailing in such collectivist countries as China and Russia, he asserts that such "centrally-controlled socialist states have no built-in advantages; on the contrary, regimentation has slowed down economic development in these countries." He cites Argentina, particularly, as a once-flourishing center of free enterprise that "socialism has destroyed."

Benjamin A. Rogge, a professor of political economy at Wabash College, is hardly euphoric over the outlook for free enterprise in the U. S. "The outlook for capitalism at this moment is anything but reassuring," he has stated. But he stresses that "among economists I see a growing respect for the market." He adds: "If you want to know where there is great admiration for the marketplace, go to the economists and intellectuals of Eastern Europe, where they have tried to do without markets."

The distressing fact to Mr. Rogge is that those who should be in the forefront, defending free enterprise and encouraging the faint hearts who despair at the unemployment-inflation dilemma, are in fact bringing up the rear. Alluding to the fortitude of major U.S. corporations in the face of periodic governmental pressures, for example, Mr. Rogge recalls a bit of Joseph Conrad. He recalls the reaction of a native girl to Lord Jim, relating that "Conrad describes this encounter between Lord Jim and the native girl by saying, 'He would have ravished her but for her timely compliance'; her reaction is pretty much the response of the businessman to the encroachments of government."

With dismay, the Wabash professor also remembers the performance of such business-supported organizations as the National Association of Manufacturers and the U.S. Chamber of Commerce in 1971, the year that President Nixon resorted —most unfortunately—to wage-price controls to "stop" inflation. "Take a look at who endorsed the coming of wage-price controls!" Mr. Rogge says. "Both the NAM and U.S. Chamber of Commerce!"

The professor adds: "The NAM is now repentant for its sins and is conducting a great advertising campaign against the very same wage and price controls. I would conclude that John Kenneth Galbraith [the left-leaning Harvard economics professor] and his friends have indeed taught the businessman well, and what they have taught him is to repeat the phrases that must eventually sound his own death knell." On a gloomy note, he concludes: "The capitalist fortress is, indeed, almost naked of defenders and is, indeed, encompassed round with a host of enemies."

* * *

It has been said that finance is too important a matter to be left to finance ministers—and indeed it has not been left to finance ministers during occasions in history of extreme financial crisis. By the same token, it can be argued that free enterprise is too important a matter to be left to the members of the National Association of Manufacturers and of the U.S. Chamber of Commerce.

Ultimately, any resolution of the great American dilemma of unemployment or inflation must begin with the country's leadership. Jimmy Carter, shortly before he took that oath of office in January 1977, told a meeting of labor leaders that "my folks have lived in Georgia—my father's family for 200 years; mine is the first generation that ever had a chance to finish high school." Mr. Carter went on to affirm before the labor officials that "I believe that anyone able to work ought to work." The audience applauded loudly. In a skeptical tone, Mr. Carter continued: "A lot of people say that if you put people back to work, then we inevitably are going to have high inflation." The soon-to-be President then produced statistics to illustrate that the unemployment-or-inflation bind hasn't always existed. "We've seen," he said, that "when Harry Truman went out of office, with great pressures on the government at that time, the unemployment rate was less than three percent and the inflation rate was less than one percent."

The statistics are accurate. Such a time did exist in Harry

Truman's America and even more recently. But it exists no more. A sensible effort can be mounted to resolve today's economic dilemma, to induce economic conditions that would once again allow low unemployment and low inflation to coexist.

Any optimism engendered by the end of the war in Vietnam, the end of Watergate or the end of the worst recession since the 1930's will rapidly dissolve, however, unless the underlying economic dilemma can be managed. As we will see in the next chapter, the economic record since those early years of price stability and scant joblessness is not encouraging.

CHAPTER TWO

The Dismal Record

The economy that Jimmy Carter inherited in January 1977 was on the mend. The long recession, which began in November 1973 and persisted until March 1975, was long past. Consumer prices, on the average, were still climbing swiftly—at an annual rate of some nine percent in January 1977. And more than seven percent of the labor force was still jobless in January 1977. But both figures represented a welcome improvement over the sort of levels that had prevailed during the preceding Republican administrations.

As recently as three years before, in early 1974, double-digit rates of inflation prevailed. Barely two years earlier, some nine percent of the labor force wanted, but could not find, work.

However, the somewhat improved economic statistics that confronted President Carter in early 1977 represented a sorry contrast with those prevailing in much of the earlier post-World War II era.

Let us, for example, travel all the way back to 1953, when another new administration, not Democratic but Republican, was settling into Washington. In the course of that year, consumer prices in the country rose by an enviable amount—only seven-tenths of a percentage point. Equally enviable were the unemployment figures. During that long-ago year, joblessness averaged less than three percent of the labor force—to be precise, 2.9 percent.

If 1953 were a most wonderful aberration in the early postwar record, we could perhaps derive, faced with the recent economic debacle, a slight amount of comfort.

Not so.

The painful fact is that 1953 was merely a particularly impressive sample of the economic good health once exhibited from year to year by those two key barometers of the state of business—unemployment and inflation. Four years earlier, during 1949, the consumer-price index actually fell 1.2 percentage points, yet unemployment averaged 5.9 percent of the labor force, far less than when Mr. Carter arrived in Washington. And four years later, during 1957, the price rise amounted to a mere 2.4 percentage points and the jobless rate was only 4.3 percent. As recently as 1965, during the White House regime of Lyndon Johnson, consumer prices rose only 1.8 percentage points and yet only 3.8 percent of the labor force was unemployed.

It is largely in the years since 1965 that the dilemma has taken shape—the evidence to suggest that the country's free-enterprise economy is no longer able to function in a manner conducive to reasonably low rates of both inflation and unemployment.

The record since that watershed year has been dismal indeed. In 1966, as American involvement in Vietnam expanded and as the long business rise that began in early 1961 rolled onward, the consumer-price increase accelerated to 3.2 percentage points. Another three-point increase occurred in 1967. The climb began to accelerate—to 4.2 points in 1968 and 6.3 points in 1969. Further sharp price jumps, extending into the double-digit range, occurred in the ensuing years, right up to the moment that White House power transferred to Mr. Carter and the Democrats.

Such steep price increases, a student of earlier postwar economic performance might suppose, would be symptomatic of an exceedingly fast-paced business environment in which workers were scarce and unemployment levels exceptionally low. Let us inspect the jobless statistics for that period.

From 3.8 percent of the labor force in 1965, national unemployment climbed, slowly at first, to as high as 6.1 percent by the end of 1970. Indeed, 1970 was a recession year in the U.S. Joblessness hovered around the six percent level during much of 1971 and 1972, even though the 1970 recession had supposedly ended and an economic recovery commenced. Joblessness dipped briefly below the five percent mark in 1973 but then the rate jumped sharply again as the long recession developed late that year. During 1975, a year during which the consumer-price rise averaged about nine percent, nearly eight million Americans were listed as unemployed. A decade earlier, the total stood at just above three million.

* * *

Clearly, the U.S. economy has been functioning poorly in recent years. And the dismal performance, it is widely agreed, has proved to be a most costly business—not only in human terms, the distress of being jobless and having to rely on the dole, but in broad economic terms that can be pinned down with some precision.

The Joint Economic Committee of Congress, in its 1976 report on the status of the national economy, contained a variety of statistics. Among these were data describing the potential economic growth lost in America because of the economy's apparent inability to function smoothly, its inability to utilize fully its available resources of manpower, industrial materials and machine-power.

"The condition of the United States economy continues to be a matter of distress to members of this committee," the report began, adding that "despite recent signs of improvement, seven million people remain out of work by official count; if discouraged and underemployed workers are included, the figure exceeds 10 million." It continued: "An estimated 60 to 75 million people in 1975 were members of families in which someone was unemployed."

The report went on to translate such unused economic resources into dollar terms: "Lost income and production since the start of the [1973-1975] recession now total some $400 billion in constant 1972 dollars, and further losses by 1980 will run in the range of $600 billion to $900 billion, depending on the speed of the recovery."

The report described the situation as "a monumental waste of national resources." It added that "every percentage point in unemployment costs the U.S. Treasury an estimated $17 billion—$12 billion in lost tax revenues and $5 billion in food stamps, unemployment insurance and other support programs."

Richard Bolling, a Democratic congressman from Missouri, succeeded the late Senator Hubert Humphrey as chairman of the Joint Economic Committee in 1977. "The econony has changed drastically," Congressman Bolling says. "Not only are prices more rigid, but wages are more rigid;

not only do we have a higher level of unemployment when we come out of a recession than we used to, we also have a greater threat of inflation, and we need a new consensus because the old one isn't good enough."

The "old consensus" for many policymakers, clearly, is the idea that America's economy will grow and prosper most effectively if it continues to be rooted in a free-enterprise environment, not wholly free of government rules, to be sure, but essentially unfettered, competitive, offering incentives in return for hard work.

The "new consensus" to which the Congressman alludes, just as clearly, reflects a rejection of the free-enterprise idea, and acceptance of the argument that the government can best run things, plan things.

Listen, for a sample of new-consensus thinking, to Ray Marshall, a Texas economist who became Jimmy Carter's Secretary of Labor. Mr. Marshall discusses the emotionally charged unemployment issue. "There are a lot of things that the private sector cannot do," he says. "That being the case, we need to get public employment programs." In effect, he is saying that the dismal economic record of recent years makes it clear that private businesses in the U.S. can't do the job, so let's have Uncle Sam take over the responsibility.

Politicians and economists are by no means the only Americans whose faith in the system has been shaken by the economy's performance. Bishop James Rausch, general secretary of the U.S. Catholic Conference, asks: "What happens to a nation that begins to accept the notion that it cannot use the talents and labor of all its people? What happens to us as a people as we watch families which have made the slow and painful climb up the economic ladder, only to be pushed down once again into poverty by the loss of a job?" They lose faith, of course, in the country's economic system.

* * *

The other half of the gloomy picture is the price scene. The number of Americans categorized as "poor" rose by 2.5 million during 1975, for example, even though wage levels climbed and unemployment declined slightly over the course of that year. In fact, the 2.5 million increase, an 11 percent addition to the ranks of the poor in America, represented the largest single rise in the 17 years that the Bureau of Census had kept track of the nation's poverty line.

The main reason for such distressing increases is that the poverty line is being continually pushed up by inflation. A family has to earn far more nowadays to be able to purchase the minimum standard of food, clothing and shelter than a decade ago. The 1975 poverty line, designated by the government, was $5,500 for a nonfarm family of four. Two decades earlier, a family earning that amount in a year was in the country's middle class. In fact, a family earning $5,500 then was earning about 20 percent above the national average.

* * *

The economy's performance—the high unemployment levels combined with the high inflation rates—particularly distresses, quite understandably, many U.S. labor leaders. So embittered is William W. Winpisinger, head of the million-member International Association of Machinists, that he recently told an interviewer: "Unemployment is the great suppressor of any leftist trend in society—it stifles dissent on the campuses, among welfare mothers, in the factories and everywhere else." Few U.S. labor leaders would go that far.

On the subject of inflation, AFL-CIO President George Meany recently charged that spiraling prices are responsible for "widespread suffering for millions of families; shattered dreams for thousands of young Americans denied a decent education or an entry job; an increase in crime, drug addiction and broken homes; the worst housing shortage in history."

The persistence of unemployment and inflation in recent years has given rise to strange developments. A man in Arlington, Virginia, recently founded an organization called "Unemployed Lib" to go along with all the other "lib" movements in the country. The group's manifesto starts out: "Unemployment is as American as apple pie. . . ."

Among the group's demands are: "There should be respect and recognition for the unemployed, who through no fault of their own find themselves jobless; there should be a lowering of the number of hours worked per week to help distribute the work; the mistaken attitude that anyone can find work if they really want should be dispelled."

An indication of the price spiral is the extent to which Americans have grown accustomed to routinely handling seemingly huge sums of money. For example, a gentleman recently dropped into a bank in Traverse City, Michigan, and presented a 100,000-mark note from Germany for exchange into dollars. Bank officials promptly took the note and paid the customer $39,700 in cash. Only later, unfortunately, did the bank officials realize that the German note had been printed in 1923 during that country's runaway inflation in which the currency finally became worthless and was abandoned. The true value of the 1923 note was estimated at less than a United States penny.

In recent years, as the U.S. economic problem has worsened, economists have even devised a "misery index" designed to reflect the combined pain stemming from joblessness and inflation. The index is compiled simply by adding together the overall rate of unemployment and the rate of increase in the consumer-price index. A general rule of thumb among economists is that things begin to get pretty uncomfortable when the index gets into double digits. Anything above the 20 mark, according to the rule, represents extreme misery, if not downright agony. In recent years, the index, unhappily, has been consistently above 10 and all too often above 20 as well.

* * *

As the economy's distressing behavior has persisted, it is not surprising that an I-told-you-so attitude has developed among some analysts long skeptical about the country's free-enterprise system. "The unusual behavior of the economy has lent support to a professional group calling themselves the 'radical' economists, or, sometimes, the 'neo-marxist' economists," observes Tilford Gaines of Manufacturers Hanover Bank. Citing high unemployment rates and climbing prices, these economists "point to the 'fact' that a capitalist economy is inherently unstable," Mr. Gaines adds. "Among those committed to a free, capitalistic economic system, there are many reasons for concern. . . . The greatest uneasiness relates to price inflation; given the rate of unemployment in the labor force and in plant utilization, the historical record suggests that consumer and wholesale prices should be declining, but they have continued to rise."

An array of other national woes is blamed on the dismal economic performance. Dr. M. Harvey Brenner of Johns Hopkins University cites studies indicating a direct relationship between high readings on the aforementioned misery index and the national suicide rate, the mortality rate for cardiovascular disease, mental health problems, alcoholism and crime. In light of recent research at Johns Hopkins and at Yale University, Dr. Brenner says, "there is now substantial evidence that trends in national economic indicators have a profound influence on the state of mental and physical health of the general population, as well as on aggression and other criminal behavior."

Some analysts also attribute widespread voter apathy in part to a sense that the economy is hopelessly malfunctioning. It is noteworthy that voter participation in national elections had been rising steadily in the early postwar years and took its first sharp drop in 1972, a time when the employment-and-inflation bind was gaining increased national attention. That year, only 55 percent of those eligible to vote actually voted.

The strategic problem posed for Uncle Sam by the dilemma, particularly by the unemployment situation, was suggested in late 1976 by Harold Lever, a British politician and a longtime leader in that country's Labour Party. Mr. Lever, a most articulate and charming admirer of the U.S. and its economy, stated bluntly that "the greatest bulwark against communism has been the degree to which the Western industrial democracies have been able to resist massive and dangerous unemployment." He went on to warn that "the greatest danger would arise if the Communists were able to claim that very heavy unemployment was the price one has to pay for a private-enterprise society."

Robert L. Heilbroner, the economist, has sounded similar warnings. Viewing not only the U.S. situation but the Western economic performance generally, he predicts that "in many nations the outcome will be the rise of authoritarian governments."

* * *

The record of recent years, as disturbing as it may be, is rendered even more distressing by comparisons with the performances turned in by some other key economies.

Lester C. Thurow, a professor of economics at Massachusetts Institute of Technology, observes that in terms of per-capita production of goods and services—in effect, the U.S. standard of living—"we have been surpassed, or are about to be, by a number of countries in Europe."

Among industrial nations, the professor notes, "Sweden and Switzerland can each claim to be more successful, with a per-capita gross national product 20 percent above ours; we have also been surpassed by Denmark and are about to be surpassed by Norway and West Germany." He concludes, gloomily, that "relative to achievement in the rest of the world, the U.S. economy no longer delivers the goods."

A study by the Stanford Research Institute, a nonprofit business research organization in Menlo Park, California, pinpoints ways in which the economic performance of many major countries has exceeded that of the U.S. in recent years.

In a recent 10-year period, for example, economic growth in the U.S.—measured in terms of the "real" GNP, or GNP adjusted for inflation—rose 4.1 percent annually. This was less than the comparable 10-year rise in such countries as Canada, with a 5.5 percent gain; Japan, with 10.2 percent; West Germany, with 4.8 percent; France, with 5.5 percent;

and even troubled Italy, with 4.7 percent. Among major Western nations, only Britain, with a meager 2.9 percent gain for the period, registered a weaker showing than the U.S.

The Stanford Research study also attempts to compare unemployment rates for various countries. This is not a simple undertaking, because such rates are compiled differently in each country. In any event, the comparisons left little question about the U.S. record. Focusing on 1975, the study found that unemployment in the U.S. worked out to 8.5 percent of the labor force.

No other country in the survey came close to that high level. Canada was closest, with a rate of 7.2 percent. In Japan, the rate was a minuscule 1.9 percent; in France, 4.3 percent; in West Germany, 4.1 percent; in Italy, 3.5 percent; and in Britain, for all its much-publicized economic sluggishness, 4.8 percent.

* * *

The U.S. fares better, at first glance, in comparisons involving the price record. The Stanford Research data show that in 1975 consumer prices in the U.S. rose, on the average, 9.1 percent. This is hardly a modest rate. If it were to continue only eight years, it would halve the value of one dollar, reducing its buying power to only 50 cents. Yet, even steeper inflation rates show up for France, Italy and Britain, whose 24.3 percent consumer-price rise during 1975 was in a most unenviable class by itself.

The American price performance is, however, somewhat deceiving. This is because, in absolute terms, many U.S. prices remain far higher than similar prices abroad. A vivid illustration of this can be found in the price of a most important economic ingredient—the price of labor.

In a recent 12-month period the hourly compensation paid to U.S. production workers rose to $6.90 from $6.33, according to an analysis prepared by the U.S. Bureau of Labor Statistics. The analysis includes comparable figures, expressed in U.S. dollar terms, for other key countries. Hourly compensation rose in Japan to $3.26 from $3.05, in France to $4.59 from $4.50 and in West Germany to $6.70 from $6.33. In each instance, the latest figure undercuts the comparable U.S. hourly-pay level. In percentage terms, the nine percent increase in the U.S. figure during the 12 months is not appreciably greater than in most of the other countries. The Japanese increase, for example, works out to a gain of about seven percent. But in absolute terms, the spread between the U.S. and Japanese pay level widens to $3.65 an hour from $3.28 an hour during the 12 months.

The analysis further shows that in two countries, Italy and Britain, the hourly pay figures, again expressed in terms of the U.S. dollar, actually fell during the 12 months—to $4.27 from $4.44 in Italy and to $3.06 from $3.26 in Britain. By no coincidence, the international value of both the Italian lira and the British pound fell sharply during the period. This is because Italian and British labor grow considerably "cheaper" when the pay levels are translated from the respective local currencies, which depreciated in the 12 months, into dollars.

The upshot of such data is that the international competitiveness of U.S. labor, and of the U.S. economy in general, clearly has been eroded. One should also note, parenthetically, that no decline occurred during the period in the value of the West German mark. Yet, starting from the same base of $6.33 an hour, the pay level in West Germany climbed 20 cents less during the 12 months than the U.S. pay level.

In sum, a close look at comparisons of the U.S. inflation record with the price performance elsewhere shows that little comfort can be derived from the fact that the U.S. price rise, in percentage terms, has not been quite as steep as in several other places.

If the U.S. economy's price data, closely scrutinized, present such a dismal picture, if the U.S. unemployment problem remains so bleak, how can U.S. policymakers possibly try to resolve the country's painful economic dilemma?

A start, we submit, would be to explore in detail the much-publicized unemployment situation, and then the price problem. For only if both these economic difficulties are carefully assessed, placed in the fullest perspective and understood, can lasting solutions, conducive to the country's free-enterprise traditions possibly be attained. Let us focus first on the matter of unemployment.

CHAPTER THREE

Understanding Unemployment

There is surely no economic statistic that grabs more headlines or is the focus of more political attention than the nation's unemployment rate—the percentage of the American labor force that wants, but is unable to obtain, work. The vast amount of interest that this single economic figure generates when it is reported each month by the Labor Department's Bureau of Labor Statistics is readily understandable.

For one thing, there is a certain degree of scariness involved. Memories of the Great Depression of the 1930's, during which joblessness reached 25 percent of the labor force, linger on. Moreover, there is always the fear that, if one's neighbor is jobless today, unemployment may hit home tomorrow.

By the same token, the unemployment rate is among the very few economic statistics that directly reflect upon an entirely human situation, and therefore, a situation readily comprehensible to the general public. The subject is laden with emotion.

If we read in *The Wall Street Journal* or in *The New York Times* that new orders for durable goods, for example, are sharply dropping, the tendency is to view the news as a somewhat arcane, insignificant bit of statistical information about the state of the economy. The average newspaper reader does not know that economic experts actually view durable-goods orders as a highly significant precursor of broad business trends—far more significant, in fact, than the movement of the much-publicized unemployment rate.

On the other hand, if we read that the unemployment rate is sharply on the rise, we take notice. Human beings are involved. The image arises of hapless breadwinners, pink slips in hand, seeking work, wondering how to continue to feed the hungry family.

Unemployment is a good subject for politicians and union leaders to talk about and for journalists to write about. It is good copy. Almost by definition, it represents an economic evil that makers of national policy must continually strive to reduce. No politician or union leader will win an election advocating increased joblessness. Nor will any editorial writer gain admiring readers by singing the praises of a high unemployment rate.

The matter of unemployment—the awful human situation that is entailed, the distressing business of a man or a woman wanting work but not finding any—is indeed a dreadful business. It would be heartless to contend that human misery is not involved.

Yet to begin to understand the overriding dilemma of the American economy—the unemployment-and-inflation bind that has developed—it is absolutely necessary that one take a long, hard, unemotional look at the matter of joblessness. If such a procedure smacks of heartlessness, so be it. The greater heartlessness, we submit, would be to accept the popular notion that the recent, painfully high rates of unemployment, alongside the corrosive inflation of recent years, constitute indisputable proof that our long-standing economic arrangements no longer work and must be abandoned.

* * *

How difficult, really, is today's unemployment problem? What can we deduce from month after month after month of high unemployment rates? What aspects of the situation are we missing? How can the matter be placed in the fullest possible perspective?

Albert H. Cox, Jr., chief economist of Merrill Lynch, Pierce, Fenner & Smith Inc., the nation's largest securities firm, provides a comment on the much-publicized unemployment rate and public understanding of it. "In my judgment," the Merrill Lynch economist says, "the true nature of today's unemployment is not understood, the statistics are not understood, and the gravity of the problem is perceived by the vast majority of people, including politicans, to be far greater than it really is."

A similar appraisal comes from Milton Friedman, a Nobel-laureate economics professor whose studies of monetary theory have earned him a wide following in the U.S. and abroad. Recalling widespread concern about high unemployment in the summer of 1975, when the economy was just starting to pull out of the long 1973-75 recession, Mr. Friedman declares: "The report that eight million persons are unemployed conjures up the image of eight million persons fruitlessly tramping the streets looking for a job. That is a false picture. Most people recorded as unemployed are between jobs or between entering the labor force and finding a job. Most are in families that have one or more other earners. Most receive some income while unemployed. Each week more than half a million find jobs, while some half-million other people begin to look for jobs."

The economist arrives at a conclusion that hardly typifies the public view, or for that matter the Washington view, of the unemployment problem. "Unemployment," he states, "is certainly a serious problem, but we must not be misled by ambiguous statistics."

* * *

An important step in gaining a fuller perspective on the nation's jobless problem is to realize that there are really many unemployment rates, not just the overall figure that grabs the headlines when it is reported by the Bureau of Labor Statistics each month. These range "on a scale from a very narrow to a very broad definition," says Julius Shiskin, a BLS commissioner who has worked extensively to improve the nation's unemployment data.

The various unemployment "indicators," as Mr. Shiskin calls them, are numbered from U-1 up to U-7. The BLS issues each indicator monthly. Briefly, they are defined as follows:

U-1 shows persons unemployed 15 weeks or longer as a percent of the total civilian labor force; U-2 shows job losers as a percent of the civilian labor force; U-3 expresses unemployed household heads as a percent of the household-head labor force; U-4 shows unemployed full-time jobseekers as a percent of the full-time labor force; U-5, the rate that grabs the headlines, gives the total unemployed as a percent of the civilian labor force; U-6 shows the jobless rate for full-time jobseekers plus those seeking part-time jobs for economic reasons; and U-7 shows what the overall unemployment rate would be if so-called discouraged workers, persons who have given up looking for work but would like a job, are included.

Julius Shiskin maintains that "even this broad array does not provide all of the possible measures" of the national labor situation. He stresses that even "the broadest measure, U-7, is a crude measure of the potential labor supply [and] does not take into account the fact that if economic conditions were very good, many persons besides discouraged workers would enter the labor force; there are perhaps millions outside the labor force who would be motivated to seek and take jobs under certain hypothetical conditions."

Data gathered by Mr. Shiskin illustrate how widely the rates of the various U's differ. At the start of 1977, for example, U-1 stood at only 2.4 percent, while the U-7 rate was up around the 11 percent level. The various U's don't even necessarily move in the same direction. In the course of 1976, U-1 inched down from 2.7 percent to 2.6 percent. But U-7 climbed during the same span from 10.2 percent to 10.7 percent.

A recent study by the Philadelphia Federal Reserve Bank underscores the complexity of unemployment data and the hazards of fixing one's attention solely on U-5, the headline-grabbing, overall rate. "The unemployment rate must be used carefully as a measure of economic health," the study cautions. It concedes that "the overall unemployment rate is a favored indicator of the economy's health—a low rate is viewed as a sign that the economy is vibrant and well, whereas a high rate is considered a signal of economic anemia."

The report then proceeds to point out that "the single percentage figure, however, doesn't show who it is that unemployment hits; nor does it tell us about the economic condition of those who are unemployed; and as an indicator of the business outlook it's often ambiguous because, contrary to popular belief, it sometimes rises when the economy is improving and falls when the economy is sagging." In conclusion, the bank states, "Getting a grip on the amount of unemployment in the economy is no easy task—there is no feasible way to add up all the people in unemployment lines."

Michael L. Wachter, an economics professor at the University of Pennsylvania, has undertaken extensive research into unemployment for the Brookings Institution in Washington. While his discussion focuses in technical language on the rightward shift of the aforementioned Phillips curve, his conclusion is plain enough. "Official unemployment," he warns, "is not an accurate measure of labor-market tightness."

* * *

One should note, parenthetically, that the official unemployment rate, while an inaccurate labor-market gauge, is not an unimportant one. All sorts of government-assistance programs are geared to the unemployment figures produced by Washington's statistics mills. For example, the Economic Development Agency, which administers many public-works programs, estimated in 1977 that Massachusetts had lost some $14 million under a $2 billion works program simply because of statistical inaccuracies that caused the state's jobless figure to be unrealistically low.

The Massachusetts case, it should be added, is something of an aberration, inasmuch as the state's unemployment rate turned out to be unrealistically low. The preponderance of evidence, as comments earlier in this chapter from Mr. Cox of Merrill Lynch indicate, is that more often than not unemployment rates are unrealistically high rather than low.

Many factors underlie this tendency. They range from demographic developments to the impact of unions on labor-force trends.

* * *

Let us look first at a development which, for all the publicity it has received in recent years, remains only dimly understood by many Americans, at least as far as its impact on the unemployment figures is concerned. This is the influx of women into the labor force in recent years. The figures documenting this trend are remarkable indeed.

At the start of the post-World War II era, slightly more than 16 million working-age women were in the country's labor force. The American population at that time contained approximately 52 million women of working age—that is, according to governmental definition, at least 16 years old. Thus, at the start of the postwar era some 30 percent of the nation's working-age women either worked or sought work.

More than three decades later, a massive increase in this labor-force participation rate is evident. Recently, some 38 million women, in a working-age population of more than 80 million females, were in the American labor force. This works out to a labor-force participation rate of nearly 50 percent.

Put another way, the country's population of working-age women over the three decades rose more than 50 percent, assuredly a healthy increase. But the number of these women wishing to participate in the labor market rose more than 130 percent.

Within some age categories, the rise in female labor-force participation has reached spectacular proportions. Among women aged 20 to 24 years old, the participation rate is nearly 65 percent, some 20 percentage points higher than in the late 1940's. The participation rate is approaching the 60 percent level even for women within the 25-to-44 age span, once regarded as a time when familial duties precluded jobholding.

A few additional statistics help to underline this remarkable influx of women into the labor force. A recent Labor Department analysis reports that 91 percent of the nation's bank tellers now are female, along with 87 percent of cashiers and bookkeepers, 74 percent of payroll clerks, 72 percent of health technicians, 54 percent of office managers, and 48 percent of insurance adjusters.

Clearly, woman's place no longer is only in the home. The highly publicized "women's liberation" movement certainly plays a part in this. But another factor, less publicized but possibly more profound, is involved as well. It is, simply, that the sort of jobs proliferating in today's highly automated, highly technological, service-oriented economy don't require brawn. Brains are the necessary prerequisite today, and the male sex long ago discerned that, in this regard, it commands no premium.

Mr. Shiskin of the BLS comments that there has been a "growing acceptability of working mothers, even for those with preschool children." He adds that "desires for a higher standard of living, and inflationary pressures, have undoubtedly encouraged the young wives to remain in the labor force and contribute to family income." The BLS official believes without question that "this rapid growth in the labor force" explains in large part why the nation's unemployment rate has remained at disturbingly high levels in recent years. The economy has simply not been able to absorb all of the influx of women who want work.

Both husband and wife now work in nearly 45 percent of all U.S. families. This is up from 29 percent as recently as 1960. In absolute terms, the number of such dual-breadwinner families stands at about 20 million, an increase of nine million in only a decade and a half. Recently, the total has been rising at a rate of some one million yearly.

* * *

Demographic factors converging to produce high rates of joblessness extend well beyond the phenomenal influx of women into the labor force.

A study by the Conference Board, the nonprofit business-research organization in New York City, warns that "unemployment is likely to remain a major problem" in coming years, even if the U.S. economy expands at a brisk clip. The explanation is simple enough, according to the Conference Board. "The labor force has been growing at an unprecedented rate, with a flood of young people seeking work," the study states. "Some 1.7 million newcomers have been entering the labor force each year since the late 1960's—and the number has been even higher recently; this is up from less than one million a year in the 1950's and early 1960's."

Fabien Linden, a Conference Board economist, predicts that "for the next two or three years, at least, the labor force will continue to expand at a rapid pace, and there will be no significant tapering off" until sometime in the 1980's. He notes that "the structure of unemployment has changed significantly in recent years, with a very high proportion of those looking for work being young people and women."

The analyst concedes that "while this group has traditionally had high unemployment rates, they are comprising a rapidly growing proportion of the labor market." He states that "the pressure to find jobs for the swelling tide of young adults has recently become more acute, and the demographic statistics suggest that the problem will persist for quite some time." His conclusion: "The concern of government policymakers that we will experience high unemployment for an extended period is based on relentless fact."

A development that Mr. Linden and other demographers stress is that, at present, almost twice as many persons are reaching working age as are reaching retirement age. This situation, population analyses indicate, will persist for many years to come.

Some economists have claimed that a trend toward earlier retirement should serve to ease the situation to a degree. This is certainly a possibility. However, there is a question about just how solid the much-publicized early-retirement trend really is. A conventional view on the matter is typified by Peter F. Drucker, a well-known author and management consultant. "With an ever greater proportion of the population in retirement, the United States faces a shortage of manual labor by the early 1980's," he maintains, adding that "businessmen should prepare for the labor shortage by creating a less rigid retirement system and by structuring more part-time jobs—full-time jobs permanently staffed by two people—that could be filled by middle-aged women whose families have grown."

However, Mr. Linden and many other analysts tend to discount such a view. "Drucker enlists dubious demographics to document his dismal prognosis," Mr. Linden contends. "For many years ahead, the retiree count will remain almost constant," the Conference Board economist estimates. He adds that the figure, notwithstanding the conclusions of Peter Drucker, "will not rise significantly until the mid-1980's."

A similar opinion emerges in an analysis of the retirement issue by New York's Morgan Guaranty Trust Company. "Over the past decade or so in this country, early retirement has become a growing way of life," the Morgan study observes. "The old standard of mandatory retirement at 65 increasingly has been liberalized to permit workers to leave the job at age 62, 60 or even sooner; corporate enticements to encourage retirement have grown—lump-sum payments, pension supplements and consulting arrangements—and added momentum has come from unions which have bargained successfully for early-retirement provisions (an autoworker recently retired at age 49)."

However, Morgan Guaranty's analysis continues: "Pressures, small yet mounting, can now be detected to bring a change in retirement practices, and this time the direction is toward later, not earlier, retirement."

Agitation for this, the bank reports, is coming from many quarters. These include healthy, energetic older workers who object to being forced out of jobs that they can still handle well and still enjoy. Other agitation can be traced to financial analysts who foresee staggering burdens in a Social Security system already severely overburdened; to economists who foresee stronger economic growth ahead for the U.S. economy, if able-bodied older citizens are encouraged to keep working; and to medical advisers who claim that enforced idleness at age 65 or younger is detrimental to the good health of the individuals being forced to retire.

Morgan Guaranty further notes that a small but rising number of corporations are starting to adopt "open-end" retirement programs wherein workers whose performance records are exceptional are encouraged to stay on beyond 65. Also, a group of advisers to the Social Security Administration has recommended a gradual increase in the "normal" retirement age to 65 and a pushing up to 65, from the present 62, of the age at which retirees can qualify for reduced Social Security pensions. Recent legislation extends mandatory retirement to age 70.

Dr. K. Warner Schaie, a gerontologist at the University of Southern California, has estimated that a "meaningful" retirement age today, in terms of a person's ability to handle full-time work, is at least 10 years higher than two decades ago. The explanation, of course, is that medical techniques have improved greatly in recent years and, in the process, produced a remarkably healthy population of 65-year-olds.

Some lawyers have recently argued that forced retirement, based solely on age and not on an individual's ability to work, is a denial of human rights under the equal-rights clause of the 14th Amendment to the U.S. Constitution. "Courts in several states have so ruled, and the matter eventually will come before the Supreme Court unless Congress acts first," predicts Morgan Guaranty.

An any event, the bank appears convinced that retirement may soon be coming later and later rather than, in the pattern of recent years, earlier and earlier. And however beneficial that may be for those workers directly affected, one result will be to place additional pressure on the nation's economy to generate enough jobs. Otherwise, there will likely be still higher levels of unemployment as jobseekers continue to flock into the labor force at rates far beyond the capacity of the economy to absorb all of them.

* * *

Surveying the various demographic trends, John W. Kendrick, an economics professor who served during the mid-

1970's as chief economist of the Commerce Department, declares: "The greater number of workers will require the creation of a larger number of jobs to reduce unemployment." Mr. Kendrick likes to discuss the problem of jobs in terms of a concept developed by another prominent economist mentioned earlier in this book, Arthur Okun. Mr. Okun devised a formula, first put forward in 1962, called Okun's law.

According to Okun's Law, an increase in the "real" gross national product of about 3.5 percent a year is required merely to keep the unemployment rate from rising. The dictum further states that each percentage-point addition to real GNP above that 3.5 percent-a-year brings a reduction in the unemployment rate of about one-third of a percentage point. For example, according to Okun's Law, a three percentage-point increase in real GNP above the base rate of 3.5 percent annually would cut the unemployment rate from, say, five percent to four percent. Mr. Okun used data from 1947 to 1960 in arriving at his conclusion.

Applying Okun's Law to the unemployment situation at the end of 1976, a year when the jobless rate averaged 7.7 percent, Mr. Kendrick found that economic growth of 6.25 percent annually would be necessary to bring unemployment comfortably below the five percent mark—to 4.7 percent precisely—by 1980. Mr. Kendrick used the latest demographic projections of labor-force growth in his calculation. A growth rate of 6.25 percent annually over four years would represent an extraordinary rate of economic expansion—more than double the economy's long-term annual growth over this century, nearly double the expansion rate that most government analysts deem comfortably in line with the U.S. economy's actual capacity to expand, considering available resources of labor and material.

A six percent-plus rate of economic growth in a year is not impossible, history shows. But such growth in the past has normally been sustained for only a couple of years, at the most. Unmistakably, experience teaches that such growth, persisting for anything approaching four years in a row, would bring on spiraling inflation in an overstrained economy long before anything approaching a 4.7 percent level of unemployment would materialize. Thus, once again, we see emerging the overriding dilemma, the economy's painful bind of high unemployment or high inflation.

* * *

On top of demographic pressures tending to push up overall unemployment is a lamentable, widespread mismatching of jobseekers and jobs. Such mismatching, however, is a part of the price that must be paid for the degree of employment freedom enjoyed in America. Unlike, say, Russian youths, young Americans are under relatively little restriction in choosing their field of training for entry into the adult labor force. By the same token, American educational institutions are largely free to fashion their courses of study as they see fit.

Desirable as all this may be, one unfortunate effect has been a tendency of the country's educational system to turn out, for example, poets and anthropologists, when well-trained appliance repairmen may be a good deal more necessary. Jack Golodner, an official of the AFL-CIO, observes that the country currently has a "surplus of college-credentialed people, relative to the number of openings that can use their skills." He puts this surplus at "one million or more" young Americans.

Areas of the economy where jobs are hard to fill include many where job training is often poor, such as appliance repair. But there also are fields where jobs are difficult to fill simply because people disdain the work. This disdain may reflect dangers involved, or the arduous nature of the jobs, or social considerations. Take the case of domestic work. By a recent count, the number of household workers in the U.S. is dropping sharply. The total now stands at about 700,000, down from 962,000 as recently as 1971. Yet, demand for household workers has risen steeply as more and more housewives have opted, as noted earlier in this chapter, to go out and seek jobs. "It's not that we are failing to train enough people for such jobs," says a Labor Department analyst. "Rather, it's that fewer and fewer people are willing, in our egalitarian society, to take on work that smacks of a menial, servant-like nature."

* * *

Governmental efforts to improve living standards of American families, ironically, also tend to aggravate unemployment. Let us first consider the matter of unemployment compensation. An editorial-page article in *The Wall Street Journal* attempts to anaylze the role that benefits paid to jobless personnel may play in the relatively high jobless rates of recent years. It states: "The ability to draw extended unemployment benefits clearly encourages some workers to stretch out, or in some cases even seek, periods of joblessness." The article goes on to cite the case of a jobless cement-industry worker, a native of Florida now residing in Philadelphia, who, among other dislikes, can't stand Philadelphia's cold winters. Accordingly, the man refuses to join a union in Philadelphia, safe in the knowledge that nonunion cement workers in the city are almost always out of work in wintertime. Jobless, he is eligible for unemployment benefits—which help him to afford wintering in his native Florida.

Obviously, it would be heartless to suggest that all recipients of unemployment compensation are chiselers who want to spend more time sitting in the sun, financed by U.S. taxpayers. A broader view of unemployment compensation comes from Janet L. Norwood, an official at the Bureau of Labor Statistics. She regards unemployment compensation as a major weapon against proliferating poverty, especially in periods of economic recession. "Under this program," she explains, "unemployed persons may receive up to 50 percent of their gross earnings, although there is considerable variation from state to state." She recalls that at the worst of the severe 1973-75 recession, when unemployment approximated nine percent, "more than 5.3 million persons were claiming benefits on regular unemployment-compensation programs and another 800,000 were claiming benefits from special emergency programs" set up to cope with the recessionary environment. The weekly benefits paid out, the BLS official reports, "range from less than $50 in Puerto Rico and Mississippi to a high of more than $90 in Illinois and the District of Columbia."

Such facts are not in dispute. Nor is the undeniable evidence that unemployment compensation does seem to mitigate family hardship in bad economic times. Still, as one recalls the Philadelphia cement worker, there can be no question that unemployment compensation, which has been sharply on the rise in recent decades, tends to push up unemployment in America. John O'Riley, a retired *Wall Street Journal* columnist, has put the situation aptly. There is surely a large "prop" to today's high unemployment rate that can't be measured, he says, adding that "nobody can ever prove statistically that it is a prop, yet it must be, and it may be a big one indeed—this is the very large flow into public pockets of nonpaycheck money." At the top of his list is unemployment compensation which, according to Mr. O'Riley, "may cause people to list themselves as unemployed when they really aren't trying very hard to get employed." In a recent decade, he notes, payments for unemployment compensation and other such nonpaycheck money quadrupled—reaching more than $200 billion.

An extreme illustration of the troubling side of unemployment compensation can be seen, among other places, in New York State, where a fight has been under way to abolish such payments to workers on strike. "To call a worker on strike unemployed, and then to compound the felony by allowing him to collect unemployment-compensation handouts, is the height of legislative stupidity," remarks one Albany legislator who has strongly opposed the bizarre arrangement—unsuccessfully—in the New York State Assembly. He adds: "Is it any wonder that, with such regulations, New York State has been saddled over the years with one of the highest jobless rates in the nation? A man on strike should not be treated as an unemployed member of the labor force."

A study by Kenneth W. Clarkson, an economist at the University of Miami's Law and Economic Center, also explores the connection between the high unemployment rates of recent years and government programs aimed at alleviating the financial distress of unemployed and poor families. Titled "Inflated Unemployment Statistics," the Clarkson study focuses on the impact on jobless rolls of work-registration requirements introduced in the early 1970's as a condition for receiving food stamps and other welfare benefits. Mr. Clarkson's research leads him to conclude that many recipients of such relief—who previously would not have done so—now profess to be seeking jobs in order to meet the work-registration rule.

The University of Miami economist estimates, for example, that in 1976 the nation's unemployment rate, adjusted to offset the impact of the work-registration requirement, amounted to 5.3 percent of the labor force. This is sharply below the official unemployment rate for 1976, as reported by the Bureau of Labor Statistics, of 7.7 percent.

* * *

Perhaps the most distressing facet of the nation's unemployment picture involves teen-agers. The jobless rate for young Americans is far far higher than for the U.S. labor force as a whole. Near the pit of the 1973-75 recession, the overall jobless rate was bad enough, approximating nine percent of the labor force. But the unemployment rate among teen-agers generally stood at about 20 percent or more than twice the overall level. For black teen-agers, the statistics are even more dismal—a jobless rate of roughly 40 percent.

One obvious effect of such extraordinarily high jobless rates for young Americans is to push up the overall unemployment level. Analyses show that teen-age joblessness in recent years has added at least a couple of percentage points to the overall average.

This in no way erases the painfulness of the general unemployment situation in the country. But it does help to show that the conventional image of a jobless American—a husky, adult breadwinner with a wife and children to support—isn't the whole picture.

It should be added, parenthetically, that unemployment among teen-agers has been rising even more rapidly in recent years than the overall rate. This is partly a demographic phenomenon—the bulging portion of the country's population made up of young people. But it clearly also reflects unwise legislative policy.

The unfortunate influence of well-intentioned legislation can be seen especially in the area of minimum-wage rules. The affection that leaders of most major U.S. labor unions hold for minimum-wage legislation hardly needs elaboration. Particularly, there is a conviction among union officials that, without an all-inclusive minimum wage that covers young labor-force members as well as adults, teen-agers inevitably will grab jobs from breadwinners.

The fear sounds logical enough. The trouble is that study after study—for instance, a recent one by the Brookings Institution in Washington—shows unmistakably that one effect of minimum-wage legislation is to exacerbate teen-age joblessness. Labor-union leaders who worry, no doubt sincerely, that exempting teen-agers from the rules would promptly lead to severe job problems for breadwinners might well ponder the fact that many countries abroad have no minimum for teen-age workers—and yet unemployment rates among adults in these countries are generally lower than in the U.S.

How can this be?

One sensible explanation, it would seem, is that teen-agers working at sharply lower pay levels do not replace breadwinners in America or anywhere else. Rather, they open up new jobs, or reopen old jobs, that simply don't get done otherwise on account of the labor costs involved. The sort of jobs that spring to mind range from raking golf-course sand traps (often visited by the author) to working in town libraries.

One such library, the Whittemore Memorial Library in Naugatuck, Connecticut, in early 1977 employed six pages at $2.31 hourly, one penny above the federal minimum wage at that time. Philip T. Paul, chairman of the library's board of trustees, recounts the impact that ever-climbing minimum-wage levels has had on the library's costs. The six pages, he explains, were used "to check out and reshelf books and to carry out various other routine tasks." He describes the teenagers' work as "clean, light, generally pleasant and it fits into after-school hours."

The spiraling cost of the pages derives directly from repeated minimum-wage increases, mandated by Washington, the library official says. "A few years ago, we paid them $1 per hour; then $1.60 per hour; then $1.91 per hour; and then $2.31 per hour," he says. He adds that assorted other "troubles" have stemmed from these mandated pay increases. "As the wages of the pages went up," he reports, "everyone else went up; the hierarchical difference must be maintained. . . . It is like a totem pole—if the low man moves up, everyone else moves up."

The upshot, Mr. Paul says, is that the library, which once delighted in affording six jobs for young people in the area, is now taking a very hard look at its budget. "Why should I hire a high school student?" says the official. Perhaps, he reckons, it is possible to scrape along with fewer pages, or, at the least, to hire "a reliable woman for the same price."

Can there be any question that teen-age unemployment in America is a dreadful problem? Or that such short-sighted legislation as minimum-wage rules encompassing teen-age workers aggravate the situation?

* * *

Pressures tending to push up overall joblessness do not, unfortunately, end with the minimum-wage rules. America is a country whose people are constantly on the move. This peripatetic characteristic provides a necessary element of dynamism in the U.S. economy. It enables change to come more easily. Switly expanding business sectors more readily acquire the personnel needed to support exceptional rates of growth. There is less of a tendency than in many countries for workers to linger on in stagnating economic sectors.

All this, obviously, is to the good. However, it does also mean that what economists call "frictional" unemployment tends to be relatively high in the U.S. Briefly defined, frictional unemployment is the inevitable joblessness that results when workers are in the process of moving from one job to another. Not always, of course, but frequently a brief period of unemployment occurs, particularly in a society whose unemployment-compensation program is, as we have seen, most generous.

A U.S. Labor Department study finds that in a recent five-year period one in three American workers gave up his job and changed his career. Indeed, the study shows that career-switching was the major reason for workers' resignations during the five-year period. Labor Department analysts also report job-hopping in other major countries, while on the rise, remains far less frequent than in the U.S.

One result, clearly, is upward pressure on unemployment. Some economists estimate, in fact, that frictional unemployment may account for as much as three percentage points in the nation's jobless rate. In other words, even if the U.S. had no unemployment problem, even if everyone who wanted a job could have a job, some 3 percent of the labor force—the job-hoppers—would still show up in Washington's data mills as unemployed.

It is noteworthy, by the same token, that Americans are particularly prone to quit their jobs. Politicians and union leaders who bemoan high unemployment levels might occasionally focus their attention on statistics that show the so-called quit rate of the U.S. labor force. Geoffrey H. Moore, a senior official at New York's National Bureau of Economic Research, a nonprofit organization, regards the propensity of American workers to quit their jobs as a particularly healthy economic sign. "It takes a hell of a lot of confidence to quit your job," Mr. Moore states, adding that he places considerable stock in the labor-force quit rate—the rate at which workers quit their jobs each month—as a yardstick of consumer confidence. He is quick to acknowledge, at the same time, that a high quit rate necessarily tends to push up the nation's unemployment level.

Also serving to aggravate unemployment is the increasing concern over preservation of a clean environment. Like job-hopping, efforts to curb industrial pollution assuredly are beneficial. However, there is no doubt that they constitute still another barrier to trimming joblessness. Robert A. Georgine, president of Building and Construction Trades Department of the AFL-CIO, voices a union leader's distress at the impact of environmental concerns on jobs. He cites, with bitterness, a recent decision by a U.S. Court of Appeals to halt "construction on the $100 million Tellico Dam Project because a three-inch perch which feeds on snails at the bottom of the Little Tennessee River has been placed by Congress on the endangered-species list." Mr. Georgine adds, sarcastically, that "no one even had heard" of the small creature when the dam was proposed. The union official contends that such environmental practices are "without justification" because of the "increased unemployment, economic adversity and human hardship" that they cause.

As Mr. Georgine's comments suggest, union leaders are deeply concerned about the nation's unemployment problem. Yet it is possible to trace a direct link between particularly high unemployment among certain types of union workers and particularly high pay rates. An excellent illustration is offered by Mr. Georgine's own construction workers. Among the highest paid in the nation, they also in recent years have suffered extraordinarily high joblessness. Indeed, as we will see in a subsequent chapter, the group's unemployment problem is prompting its leaders, such as Mr. Georgine, to temper pay demands.

Generally, however, union pay levels have continued to push relentlessly upward, despite high jobless rates. The apparent attitude of union leaders in many cases is that they would rather have a relatively small number of exceedingly well-paid members than a larger but less highly paid membership.

This union attitude is still another reason that unemployment in recent years has been so persistently high, in good times as well as in bad times. As we will see in the next chapter, there is another side to the labor-force coin, a much brighter side that deserves our full attention but, unfortunately, all too often fails to get it.

CHAPTER FOUR

Proliferating Jobs

A humor magazine that delights in poking fun at apparent stupidities committed in the press, the Washington bureaucracy and the executive suites of big business once pounced upon what seemed a marvelously funny blunder by statisticians of the U.S. Labor Department. In their monthly report showing labor-force developments, the magazine observed, the Labor Department statisticians had come up with a most amusing incongruity—namely, the news that in the preceding month, a month during which unemployment rose steeply across the nation, employment also climbed sharply, more sharply in fact than the increase in joblessness.

A substantial number of people who happened to spot that little item of intended humor in the magazine no doubt found the Labor Department's report laughable indeed. But anyone closely familiar with the country's labor situation would have recognized immediately that the Labor Department numbers were eminently bona fide. Only persons ignorant of America's labor paradox, such as, apparently, the magazine's editors, could possibly believe that Washington's statisticians were blundering.

This paradox that escapes so many casual observers of the country's labor scene is simply explained. Just as there is a well-publicized, gloomy aspect to the labor-force data—the unemployment rate discussed in the previous chapter—so there is a relatively little-noticed, very happy aspect: the remarkable proliferation of jobs throughout the nation.

Julius Shiskin of the Bureau of Labor Statistics, as well as other noted economists, has occasionally tried to focus attention on this happy situation by using the analogy of a doughnut. Americans have tended over the years, the official contends, to pay considerable attention to the "hole" in the labor-force doughnut—the unemployment rate. However, he goes on, the thing that one should really be examining, the part of the labor-force doughnut that really counts, is the "ring"—the number of actual jobs that exist and provide earnings for individuals.

If unemployment attracts excessive attention, the argument runs, employment, the ring of the doughnut, the bright side of the coin, attracts too little.

Milton Friedman, the economist, likes to talk not of the unemployment rate but of something he calls the employment ratio. Put simply, the employment ratio is the percentage of the nation's working-age population that holds a job.

Like many economists, Mr. Friedman is convinced that the employment ratio offers a much clearer, truer picture of America's labor scene than the unemployment rate. "The number of people unemployed is not a hard number," the University of Chicago economist says. "It depends on the answer, in a sample survey, to the question: Has any member of this household been looking for work during the past four weeks?" The answer, he goes on, may well depend on such uncertainties as the availability of unemployment benefits.

If they are not available, he explains, people who do not really want a job have no incentive to look for work. But if eligibility for benefits depends on being available for employment, such people do have a strong incentive to go through the motions of looking for work. He cites the extreme case of a professional baseball player who collects unemployment compensation during the off-season. The availability of unemployment compensation, he adds, establishes "an incentive for people who might otherwise not be in the labor force at all to take a job in order to qualify" for such compensation later on.

Mr. Friedman's observations, it should be noted in passing, are buttressed by evidence assembled by Mr. Clarkson of the University of Miami, mentioned in the preceding chapter, that various jobless benefits are tending to inflate overall unemployment.

"Unemployment is a serious and important problem," Mr. Friedman concedes. "But emphasis on the single unemployment percentage, as if it were meaningful and homogeneous, gives a misleading impression of both the nature of the problem and its magnitude."

* * *

Let us briefly ponder at this point, with a specific illustration, the sort of situation in which employment climbs along with unemployment. Take September of 1974. During that month, the nation's overall unemployment rate climbed from 5.4 percent of the labor force to 5.8 percent, suggesting a clear deterioration in the country's labor situation. However, figures put out by the Bureau of Labor Statistics also show that employment rose appreciably during the month, from 86,187,000 to 86,538,000, an increase in jobholders of some 350,000 in 30 days.

The paradox can be readily explained. The number of persons entering the labor force and seeking jobs rose extra-steeply in that month. The percentage of the country's working-age population holding jobs or seeking work rose during the month from 61.7 percent to 62.1 percent. In such percentage terms, the increase may not seem great. However, it translates into an increase in America's total labor force of roughly 800,000 individuals. A major factor, of course, was the continuing flow of women from the home to the office, a persistent trend explored in the previous chapter.

"The unemployment rate has become a misleading statistic," says Geoffrey Moore of the National Bureau. This is because, he says, "at the same time that it is at a high level, the percentage of the population employed is also at a relatively high level." The economist observes that the aforementioned employment ratio "is known to almost no one and consequently is virtually ignored in evaluations of the employment situation." As Mr. Moore puts it, "the unemployment statistics prevail."

The National Bureau analyst finds this "doubly unfortunate." He is convinced that the employment figures are actually sounder statistics than the unemployment data. As he notes, so-called discouraged workers–individuals who have unsuccessfully sought work for so long that they have given up searching and dropped out of the labor force–are excluded from unemployment figures because to be officially "unemployed" one must be jobless and actively seeking work. However, the statistical problem of taking these discouraged workers into account obviously does not arise when the country's labor situation is gauged by means of the employment ratio.

"The moral isn't that we should abandon the unemployment statistics," the National Bureau economist says. However, he continues, "they are not sufficient unto themselves. The employment figures should get just as much attention, especially in evaluating the need for public policies to provide jobs, or assessing the effectiveness of existing policies." Specifically, he urges that "the employment ratio not be ignored in measuring the tightness of the labor market and the position of the economy with respect to the goal of full employment without inflation."

To illustrate how looking at the economy's performance through this perspective can alter one's impression, it is instructive to consider, for example, the labor-force scene during the early months of 1977. In the first quarter of that year, although the economy had been in a recovery phase of the business cycle for some two years, the overall jobless rate remained stubbornly above the seven percent level. Concern over unemployment and insufficient job creation was widespread in Washington and on main streets throughout the country. Yet, if anyone took the time to study employment data in that period, it would have been readily apparent that the country's reserve labor was actually extraordinarily low. The employment ratio was near the 60 percent market, considerably higher in fact than in some earlier post-World War II decades when overall joblessness was down comfortably in the four percent area.

By no coincidence, the percentage of the country's working-age population not actually working was near a record low. Indeed, it was lower, for this particular stage of the business cycle, than ever before.

Seen through the lens of employment data, the country's labor scene in early 1977 was positively radiant. The American economy, though repeatedly accused in the press and elsewhere of woeful sluggishness, was in reality generating jobs at an admirable, even awesome, clip.

A few more statistics help to bring into still sharper focus this brighter side of the labor-force coin.

During a recent 10-year period, the U.S. population rose 10 percent, a considerable increase amounting in absolute terms to some 20 million persons. However, in the same 10 years, the number of jobholders across the nation surged by 21 percent. That percentage, placed in long-term perspective, is quite dramatic. In the previous 10-year period, the number of jobholders rose only 14 percent, and in the 10 years before that, in the early post-World War II era, the increase amounted to only 12 percent.

Altogether, such historical data show that job growth in the U.S., far from stagnating in a supposedly sluggish economy, has actually accelerated in marked fashion. It is most certainly a brighter picture of business activity than can possibly be gleaned from the unemployment figures. It is also, we submit, a much more accurate picture of the postwar economic record.

"The American economy has generated substantial opportunities for employment in the past 15 years," declares a study by economists of Harris Trust and Savings Bank in Chicago. The analysis adds that "prospects for employment increases in the next few years are quite favorable."

Julius Shiskin shares such optimism. He also subscribes to the view expressed by other economists that, as he puts it, "employment is a firmer and more objective concept than unemployment." He concludes that "the employment-to-population ratio seems to be one of the best measures of economic performance" available to U.S. policymakers. Along the same line, Norman Robertson, economist of Mellon Bank in Pittsburgh, remarks: "The unemployment rate, in and of itself, has now become a rather misleading measure of the nation's economic health."

It should be noted, parenthetically, that the proliferation of jobs in recent years has been even more pronounced than the rise in jobholders indicates. Bureau of Labor Statistics estimates show that about six percent of men who work hold more than one job and about three percent of working women are multijobholders. In absolute terms, that amounts to some five million additional jobs—jobs not readily apparent in a simple head count of the nation's work force.

* * *

The country's labor picture is brighter still if one considers several other aspects of the situation. One involves the armed forces. For whatever reason, Labor Department statisticians choose to consider only civilian jobs when they calculate the nation's jobless rate each month. If military jobs were taken into account as well, the unemployment rate would be appreciably lower. Obviously, there is no "unemployment" in the military services. And the number of jobs existing there is by no means an insignificant quantity. Even with America at peace, the total approximates two million.

A still more lamentable problem with the Labor Department's data is the absence of statistics that reflect unfilled jobs.

The precise number of jobs available at a given time simply isn't tabulated by the Bureau of Labor Statistics—or, for that matter, by any other data-gathering arm of the government or of private industry. The BLS is the agency that would, in the Washington order of things, be expected to make such a calculation. To do so, BLS analysts would have to measure jobs that go begging each month, just as they now conduct a monthly survey to pinpoint joblessness. The undertaking is assuredly feasible, BLS officials say. Indeed, a brief effort was made in 1969 and in the early 1970's to do just that.

As far as it went, the effort was a success. However, the undertaking was abandoned because government officials deemed that, to be performed in sufficient detail to allow would-be employers to locate potential employees, it would entail too great an expense for the Bureau's limited budget. That judgment, as it happens, was made by a Republican administration, under Richard Nixon. The Nixon team at the time was battling—unsuccessfully as it turned out—to curb double-digit inflation through, among other measures, trying to hold down expenditures within the federal bureaucracy.

It should be noted that the Republican decision to discontinue job-vacancy data was warmly greeted within the leadership of organized labor. Predictably, with its perennial campaign of criticism that the U.S. unemployment rate is too high, the labor movement hardly appreciates any statistical evidence to the effect that thousands of jobs are unfilled and going begging.

Julius Shiskin is convinced that a detailed job-vacancy report would help to fill job vacancies and at the same time reduce U.S. unemployment. But he says that such a detailed report would cost the government "many millions" annually and "we simply don't have the money." A private economist put the price tag, in 1976, at no less than $15 million, and inflation has doubtless brought that figure up considerably since then. Yet, even $20 million or more hardly seems a colossal sum alongside the multibillions involved in tax-and-spending moves that both Republican and Democratic politicians annually seem to depend upon to cut joblessness. The cost of the abandoned job-vacancy report amounted to about $1 million each year.

A Labor Department study of job-vacancy data in other countries suggests that American officials have a good deal to learn in this respect. It states, in part, that "Western European countries have done much more than the United States in the area of job-vacancy information. . . . In Sweden and Germany, interarea mobility [of jobseekers] is facilitated by comprehensive daily and weekly employment service bulletins listing job vacancies and job seekers; for professional persons and executives, Germany and Great Britain have a special placement office serving the entire nation." In Japan, moreover, the government goes so far as to maintain a computerized network of 700 offices that link up to provide job-vacancy information to a so-called national Labor Market Center.

There is much other evidence of vast numbers of unfilled jobs, unnoticed in the general concern about the unemployment figures. One need only flip through page after page of help-wanted ads in *The New York Times* each Sunday; the variety of unfilled jobs advertised there range from computer programmers to housemaids. So huge is the quantity of jobs abegging across the nation that a lengthy book was recently published titled *The Hidden Job Market*. The authors maintained, on the basis of extensive research, that some 85 percent of jobs available never even show up in the classified ads.

Still another indication of unfilled jobs amid high joblessness can be found in a report issued by the Conference Board. It is a monthly index of the volume of help-wanted advertising appearing in major U.S. newspapers. While the index did indeed decline during much of the 1973-75 recession, for example, the drop was by no means as precipitous as that slump's soaring unemployment rate might have led one to expect. Even at the worst of that recession, with unemployment in the neighborhood of nine percent of the labor force, the Conference Board's help-wanted index was only moderately dropping. And, soon after the ensuing recovery, a brisk rise in the index materialized.

Still another sign of the worker shortage in some occupations is the soaring cost of hiring. In a recent six-year span, the consumer-price index rose 44 percent, but the cost of housemaids jumped, on the average, 65 percent. That occupation, moreover, is clearly not one where a labor shortage could possibly be blamed on inadequate educational facilities.

* * *

The thrust of this chapter thus far can be readily summarized. The economy can and does generate jobs at a rate hardly to be suspected on the basis of unemployment data.

Before leaving the matter there, however, one should perhaps also attempt to place America's labor scene in the broadest possible worldwide perspective. Much has been said and written to the effect that most relatively advanced economies manage far better than America to cope with the worldwide problem of unemployment. The clear implication has been that economic policymakers abroad somehow have succeeded, at least on the labor front, where their U.S. counterparts in Washington have failed dismally.

But is this really so?

Certainly, as noted earlier in this chapter, a strong argument can be made that many foreign policymakers have gone much further than Uncle Sam in providing job-vacancy details which, in turn, serve to combat unnecessary joblessness. In addition, official unemployment-rate levels generally have remained lower abroad than in the U.S., through good economic times as well as bad.

In many instances, however, relatively low rates abroad reflect simply differences in the way that unemployment is defined in particular countries. In early 1977, for example, roughly five percent of Britain's labor force was unemployed, according to official British figures. However, a leading British economist reckons that the rate would have been actually around seven percent of the labor force or even higher, if U.S. procedures of measuring unemployment had been used. He notes that the British method counts as unemployed only those who "register"—that is, take the trouble to inform British government officials of their jobless status. This results in a significantly narrower number of jobless, this British analyst claims, than would be the case if a U.S.-type survey technique of measuring were used.

In addition, British officials occasionally play with the country's unemployment statistics in a seemingly highhanded manner that would surely produce howls of protest if a similar procedure were attempted in America. In early 1976, for instance, British officials unilaterally decided to remove from the country's unemployment roles some 127,000 job-seeking adults who also happened to be students. *The Economist*, the British weekly magazine of business news and commentary, branded the move an act of "political convenience" at a time when rising joblessness was becoming an embarrassment to the nation's authorities. Along the same line, it is noteworthy that other research shows a decidedly higher employment-to-population ratio in the U.S.—despite its relatively high unemployment rates—than in most industrial countries.

During a recent 12-month period, according to a BLS analysis, America's employment ratio was appreciably higher than the comparable ratios in such relatively low-unemployment nations as France, West Germany and Italy. Indeed, among the major powers, only Japan, with its extraordinarily low unemployment rates, boasted a higher employment ratio than America. Italy's employment ratio, at about 44 percent, was nearly 15 percentage points under the corresponding U.S. figure.

Another aspect to the foreign labor scene, at least in much of Western Europe, involves the question of migrant workers. In the mid-1970's, workers imported from such countries as Yugoslavia and Turkey comprised 28 percent of Switzerland's labor force, 10 percent of West Germany's, nine percent of France's, and seven percent of Belgium's. When business activity tended to contract in these countries, many of these migrant workers returned to their homelands. As a result, unemployment in the respective West European areas increased far more slowly than would have been the case under similar economic circumstances in, say, the U.S. Indeed, a case can be made that if America had a similar army of migrant workers who conveniently went to their native countries every time business soured, instead of onto the unemployment rolls, U.S. unemployment rates in recent years might have been the envy of at least some other countries.

In sum, the American labor scene tends to get what is called in Brooklyn, among other places, a bum rap. The U.S.

record on unemployment is not as awful as often supposed. And the employment side of the coin, much neglected, is positively bright. Unhappily, the same sort of generalizations cannot be made about patterns on the price front. Inflation, as painful as it clearly is, constitutes an even larger economic problem than is generally imagined.

CHAPTER FIVE

Understanding Inflation

Unless you are unemployed yourself, unemployment is always something awful that has happened elsewhere. Your neighbor lost his job. Or your friend's friend lost hers. Unemployment is such a shame. But it only hurts deeply—is more than simply a shame—when it hits home, when you or someone in your immediate family is the person whose job has evaporated.

Inflation is different. It visits all our homes. It troubles all of us. It is not simply something unpleasant that has afflicted the family down the street. Inflation afflicts us all—some much more severely than others. Only the precise degree of pain varies.

Inflation, in the final quarter of the twentieth century, is ubiquitous. Unemployment is a nasty, widespread problem for U.S. policymakers. But inflation permeates all aspects of the nation's social and economic climate.

What, really, do we mean by inflation? How does it originate? How, exactly, does it affect our lives?

Inflation, says Tilford Gaines of Manufacturers Hanover, is the result of "misdirected fiscal and monetary policy."

Budget deficits, underwritten by the Federal Reserve, create demand for goods and services, he observes, "without at the same time adding to the supply of these goods and services." Simultaneously, the bank economist continues, "the tendency toward inflation resulting from these policies is complemented by public attitudes toward business that discourage new investments needed to meet growing demand."

Mr. Gaines adds a warning: "Once inflation has become deeply imbedded in the economic structure, the process of unwinding it must necessarily be a lengthy one. The existing set of attitudes must be replaced by a new set which, in turn, can be developed only if there is credible evidence that inflation is coming under control."

* * *

In common usage, the term "inflation," in the press and on television, has come to mean, simply, rising prices. However, as Henry Hazlitt, a noted private economist, has observed, "Strictly, the term 'inflation' should refer only to an increase in the stock of money." Mr. Hazlitt concedes that "a rise of prices is a usual consequence of that increase, though the price rise may be lower or higher than the money increase." He maintains that insistence on the distinction is "not merely pedantic." The problem arises, he says, "when the chief consequence of an inflation is itself called the inflation." In that situation, he says, "the real relation of cause and effect is obscured or reversed."

The "inflation" that grabs headlines, worries politicians and is monitored most closely by living-cost-conscious labor leaders can be observed in the movement of the consumer-price index, or the CPI. Issued monthly by the Bureau of Labor Statistics, the CPI is a statistical measure of change in the prices of goods and services typically purchased by consumers. Essentially, explains a BLS economist, the CPI measures the purchasing power of consumers' dollars by comparing what a sample "market basket" of goods and services costs currently against what the same sample cost at various earlier dates. "The market basket," the analyst elaborates, "includes the most important goods and services purchased by the urban population and a representative sample of less important items; the market basket is thus representative of all goods and services customarily purchased" by consumers.

The CPI covers prices of food, clothing, automobiles, homes, furnishings, appliances, fuel, drugs, recreational goods, legal and medical fees, haircuts, transportation, various repair services, utility charges, insurance and sales and real-estate taxes. In calculating the index, BLS statisticians measure the change in each item's price since the previous period; these changes are averaged together, weighted according to their estimated economic importance. Though the precise numbers vary year to year, in 1977, for example, prices were obtained from roughly 21,000 widely varied establishments across the U.S., ranging from department stores to filling stations to doctors' offices to barber shops. Rent information was collected, as well, from some 16,000 tenants. These outlets and households were located in 85 metropolitan areas or cities around the country.

All sorts of union contracts, as well as various retirement payments, are geared in one way or another to changes in the CPI. According to a calculation made in 1976, a one percent increase in the CPI would automatically trigger $1 billion in additional payments to some 50 million Americans, including union members in private industry, postal employees, retired military personnel, federal civil servants and their survivors and Social Security and food-stamp recipients. "When dependents are taken into account," estimates a BLS official, "somewhere in the neighborhood of one-half of the population are directly affected by changes in the consumer price index."

* * *

Mr. Shiskin observes, quite appropriately, that "with inflation a major economic problem of today, the stakes involved in an accurate consumer-price index are very great." He remarks that there are three basic uses of the CPI—as an indicator of inflation, as a "deflator" of other indexes that must be adjusted to strip away "growth" merely reflecting higher prices, and as an "escalator" by means of which wage-earners may attempt to preserve the purchasing power of their pay gains.

The BLS official cautions that the CPI does not immediately reflect changes in expenditure patterns, nor can it immediately adjust to the introduction into the economy of new products or services. For example, he says that "the increased use of convenience foods and the rise of fast-food eating places were a well-advertised phenomenon before they could be adequately reflected in the index." Similarly, he continues, "A product which has fallen from public favor—either because its place is taken by a better product, or simply because of a change in fashion or consumer performance—may continue for a time to carry a disproportionate weight in the index until it can be appropriately phased out."

The CPI, Mr. Shiskin emphasizes, does not attempt to delineate "changes in the style of living" of Americans. It simply measures, as he puts it, "the changes in prices for a scientifically selected sample of goods and services [running] the gamut from bread and butter to television and bowling fees, from prenatal and obstetric services to charges for funeral services, from popular paperbacks to college textbooks." The CPI, he adds, "never has been limited to price changes of so-called necessities."

Examples of quality-adjustment changes within this index of inflation can be seen in its new-car component. Taken into account along with the actual auto price, according to Mr. Shiskin, are "structural and engineering changes which affect safety, the healthfulness of the outside environment, reliability, performance, durability, economy, carrying capacity, maneuverability, comfort and convenience." While it was originally felt that antipollution equipment on automobiles did not represent an increase in quality because usefulness to the purchaser was difficult to determine, it was later concluded by BLS statisticians that the devices did represent quality improvement. Consequently, quality adjustments are now made for additions of pollution controls to automobiles.

It should be noted as well that certain kinds of quality adjustments are not taken into account in compiling the CPI each month. These include, says Mr. Shiskin, "changes in style or appearance designed solely to make the product seem new or different, such as trim and configuration—unless these features were previously offered as options and were purchased by a large proportion of customers." The BLS, the official maintains, is continually researching better methods to measure quality changes.

* * *

A recent analysis by economists of Pittsburgh National Bank emphasizes the importance of the consumer-price index as a yardstick of inflation in the U.S. and praises the

BLS for "setting out what the index does and does not represent." This candor, however, "has not prevented a widespread misconception from developing—namely, that the CPI can be interpreted to show whether people's income goes as far as it used to," the bank analysis states.

There are a great many caveats about interpreting movements of the CPI, the bank's study stresses. For all the efforts of the BLS, the market basket of goods contained in the index remains "fairly narrow," the bank claims. Moreover, it finds that "changing consumption patterns" have not been promptly monitored. In summary, the analysis states, "We really do not have a very useful short-term measure of inflation."

Still, the CPI is probably as sound a gauge of inflation as exists in any country. It is undoubtedly a far more accurate measure than its counterpart in most lands. Surely, the dedication to accuracy, and the apolitical attitude, of U.S. government statisticians is to be admired.

For a glimpse of what transpires elsewhere, consider Brazil. Several years ago, when roaring inflation had become exceedingly embarrassing for that South American country's political leaders, they simply dictated the removal of housing from the Brazilian consumer-price index. It so happened that housing prices at the time were particularly fast-rising. By no coincidence, with housing removed, Brazil's price index soon began to climb more slowly. Nothing really had changed, of course, except that the populace, uninformed of the removal, imagined that inflation was beginning to moderate in their country.

* * *

It is not essential that a person seeking a broader understanding of America's inflation-unemployment dilemma thoroughly understand all ways in which the inflation part of the problem can be precisely gauged. As noted earlier, the government has devised many ways of measuring joblessness—the many "U's" described in a previous chapter. The government also has many ways of trying to pinpoint developments on the price front. The CPI method has been discussed here at some length chiefly because, like the overall unemployment rate, it is the price index that grabs the most attention and tends to influence such important matters as the cost-of-living adjustments to be made each year in key labor contracts, retirement programs and the like.

Inflation is also measured through more than a dozen other gauges. One worth noting is the wholesale price index, or the WPI, which attempts to pinpoint changes in prices of goods before they arrive at retail outlets; for this reason, the WPI tends to presage consumer-price trends. Another price index of note is something dubbed the GNP price deflator. Unlike the monthly CPI or WPI, the price inflator comes out only quarterly, but it aspires to cover a broader range than the others; indeed, it attempts to reflect all price changes occurring within the gross national product, the country's broadest yardstick of economic activity.

Over the long term, movements of the various inflation gauges tend to be parallel. In 1974, for instance, when the GNP deflator rose 10 percent, the CPI rose some 11 percent. In any event, for the interested layman, and for the purposes of this book, the CPI seems the logical index to use in discussing price developments. It is our best reflection—though assuredly it is imperfect—of the trend of our daily living costs. Accordingly, the term "inflation" can be assumed here to be synonymous with the behavior of the CPI.

* * *

Is inflation really such a bad thing?

Of course, there is the argument, occasionally expressed by economists, that a little bit of inflation is a good thing for us. After all, this theory holds, a modest degree of inflation is the price of business prosperity. When economic activity is briskly on the rise, with unemployment at a relatively low level and factories humming along close to capacity, some upward pressure on prices is inescapable, it is sometimes claimed.

In this particular view, a little bit of inflation is indeed a good thing, inasmuch as it signifies good times. It is too easy, perhaps, to disparage such an argument. The response occasionally is made that the idea of comfortably having a little inflation around all the time is approximately as realistic as comfortably being a little bit pregnant for nine consecutive months. But a moderate degree of inflation doesn't always necessarily lead to deep economic distress.

A serious objection to the little-inflation idea can be found, however, in the economic record. In the years since World War II, the early 1960's stand out as a time of relatively healthy prosperity. Unemployment fell sharply. The economy kept expanding at a brisk pace. Corporate profits climbed. Stock prices, after a sharp decline around the time of the Cuban missile crisis, rose substantially. Housing starts soared. Factory output increased steadily. After an initial sluggishness, company outlays for new production expanded strongly. Personal income of all sorts—from the hourly pay of factory workers to the dividend receipts of stockholders—climbed at a smart pace.

What happened on the price front?

The consumer-price index remained virtually flat. In some months, it rose a fraction of a percentage point. In other months, it fell slightly. Not until 1965 did the index begin to move clearly, relentlessly upward.

The long economic expansion of the 1960's, which began in 1961, lasted well beyond 1965, until nearly the end of the decade. But it is significant that the healthiest, steadiest overall economic growth occurred during the relatively early no-inflation years, rather than in the latter half of the decade when inflation was worsening.

The record book, one should add, contains some post-World War II years in which the opposite of inflation—deflation, or falling prices—occurred.

These years include, for example, 1954. The CPI fell one percent over the course of that year. Yet, 1954 was a time of recovery from a business recession. Unemployment during 1954 fell from a high of more than six percent to less than five percent at the year's end. The record suggests that in 1954, as at other times in the economic past, a little bit of inflation was in no way essential to a brisk improvement in the general economic performance.

Economic historians have managed to construct rough estimates of price trends going back over 100 years—much further back than any available unemployment records. This historical data tells the same story as the relatively recent postwar records—that prosperity can and does frequently occur without a concurrent dose of inflation.

Obviously, the consumer price index does not go back

many hundreds of years. But it does go back as far as 1913. Before that, cruder indexes of the movement of wholesale prices existed. The CPI record over the years since 1913 can be seen, among other places, in a publication called the *Historical Chart Book of the Federal Reserve System.* It shows, unmistakably, that inflation is no newcomer to the economic scene. In 1913, the CPI stood at approximately 30 percent of the 1967 average of 100. By 1920, the index had climbed to nearly 80 percent. A long decline ensued, so that as late as 1940, after a decade of the Great Depression, with its 25 percent jobless rate, the index was barely above the 40 percent mark. With the advent of World War II, and its much faster economic tempo, the CPI began a sustained period of increase. By the early 1950's, it had crossed the 80 percent mark. The climb continued, interrupted only by brief periods of flatness, such as the early 1960's mentioned earlier. After 1965, inflation began in earnest. In some years since then, as we have seen, the annual rates of increase have crossed into double-digit territory.

To place a 10 percent increase in living costs in perspective, it may be useful to consider briefly what economists call the Rule of 70. Take the annual rate of price increase—for example, 10 percent. Then divide that rate—again, 10 percent—into the number 70. The answer—in this instance, seven—is the number of years in which the dollar in your pocket would be worth half its current value if the inflation rate were to continue unabated. In short, if prices should rise at an annual rate of 10 percent for seven consecutive years, the purchasing power of a dollar bill would be chopped in half.

* * *

Inflation, notwithstanding its corrosive effect on purchasing power, is by no means an unmitigated evil. Farmers often complain that inflation has driven up the cost of such essential farm items as tractors. Far more important to their financial status, however, is the effect that inflation has been exerting on the value of their farms. In a recent five-year period, the value of American farmland doubled, a considerably faster rate of increase than that of U.S. living costs in general in the same interval. In a recent 12-month span, the U.S. Department of Agriculture reports, the average market value of an acre of agricultural property jumped to $445 from $380. In some states, the average per-acre price of farmland ranges as high as $3,000.

Underlying this great surge in the value of farmland are several factors. Land, whether farmland or land of another variety, cannot be reproduced. It is in limited supply at a time when demand, along with the U.S. population, has been on the increase. The rudimentary economics of limited supply and burgeoning demand point inevitably to higher prices. In addition, of course, farmland is doubly valuable because it can be used to produce food at at time when world food supplies appear increasingly under strain. It is productive, and therefore especially valuable, land.

Farmers, of course, aren't the only beneficiaries of inflation. Homeowners generally have tended to benefit over the post-World War II years from spiraling home prices Again, they have benefited from the fundamental economic squeeze of a limited supply of homes and sharply rising demand as new families have formed.

American homeowners also benefit from inflation to the extent that they have borrowed to buy their homes and, later, have been able to repay their mortgage loans in cheapened dollars. Indeed, any heavy borrower would tend to benefit from this aspect of inflation. As the Rule of 70 shows, the loss in value of the dollar due to inflation of 10 percent or so a year is considerable indeed. For borrowers, it could easily more than make up for the cost of paying interest. Interest charges on home loans, moreover, are limited by law and may normally be deducted from income tax payments.

While homeowners do benefit from inflation to the extent that the value of their homes has generally soared, it is unlikely, if a poll were taken, that many would come out foursquare in favor of still more inflation. Indeed, most Americans in recent years have become increasingly aware that inflation is a reason for major concern. The full dimensions of inflation's darker side are only beginning to be understood. The next chapter will sketch the extent to which inflation, far from being an economic blessing, in fact generates severe social and economic problems.

Just as the country's unemployment problem is not as large as one may be led to believe, the problem of rapidly rising prices, we will see, is a good deal more severe than one would imagine. Only if this darker side of inflation is understood can the country begin to resolve the economic dilemma that continues to bedevil policymakers.

CHAPTER SIX

Inflation's Dark Side

Like the proverbial road to hell, the road to inflation all too often is paved with good intentions. We saw in the previous chapter that inflation does occasionally benefit some people in special ways. However, the ways in which inflation inflicts social and economic harm far outweigh any benefits it may occasionally bestow.

The relentless mathematics of the Rule of 70, outlined in the previous chapter, suggest the corrosive impact of rising prices over a prolonged period. To discover that prices rise, say, seven percent in a year somehow seems less painful than to find that prices are rising at a rate that will cut the dollar's value in half in a decade.

The continual rise of prices over a prolonged period is "without a doubt the paramount problem facing America today and, for that matter, the free world," declares a study by the Industrial National Bank of Rhode Island.

Former President Ford expressed a similar point of view in a 1975 speech: "I deeply believe that our nation must not continue down the road we have been traveling [for] down that road lies the wreckage of many great nations of the past."

Inflation has been called the cruelest of all taxes. It hurts, as we have seen, the poor and the middle class far more than the very rich and powerful. It is a hidden tax, inasmuch as the unsophisticated often hardly realize it is being paid.

"Program after program is introduced to benefit one segment or another of the population," states the Industrial National Bank analysis. But "in the meanwhile the money is extracted from the people's back pocket in the form of rising taxes and, worst of all, in the form of inflation, the cruelest tax of all." The bank stresses that "the politicians are not solely to blame; if one asks any group of citizens whether they would favor cutting out a number of the 1,009 domestic-aid programs, the answer would almost unanimously be yes, but if you were to select 150 programs from the list and ask the same group whether any one of the selected programs should receive increased federal spending, 80 percent would doubtless" say yes again. "We cannot go on helping more and more people who cannot help themselves," the study concludes, because the result is merely more severe, more harmful inflation, not improved social and economic circumstances.

During a recent 16-year period, according to a report by the Conference Board in New York, an American family of four had to increase its annual pre-tax income to more than $19,000 from $10,000 simply to maintain the purchasing power. Reviewing such statistics, Tilford Gaines of Manufacturers Hanover remarks: "To the extent that money and credit creation exceeds the ability of the economy to produce real goods, all we buy is inflation—we don't add a single worker to the employed labor force; we don't add a single unit of production to the output of the economy; all we add is higher prices." In the process, he observes, families must sharply increase their earnings simply to keep their buying power from shriveling.

Many American families, of course, have managed to increase their income sharply during the last decade or two. Indeed, many families doubtless have managed actually to outrace inflation and increase their buying power. But most Americans have not kept abreast of inflation. And the unfortunate fact is that, all too often, these losers to inflation are least able to fend for themselves within our social system.

* * *

It is ironic that governmental policies aimed at aiding old persons, the sick and handicapped and the poor have tended over the decades to fuel inflation, and that inflation has ultimately hit such persons especially hard. It is deeply ironic that inflation has served over the years to widen, rather than to close, the gap between America's rich and poor. Recently, according to the U.S. Census Bureau, 24.3 million Americans —more than 10 percent of the country's population—were classified by government analysts as poor. As noted in Chapter Two, the number of Americans below the poverty line soared by 2.5 million during the single year of 1975. Around the same time, however, the economics unit of *U.S. News & World Report*, the weekly news magazine, estimated that "inflation and generally rising standards of living are creating record numbers of millionaires in this country." In a short two years, the report indicated, the number of people with net assets of $1 million or more jumped from 180,000 to about 240,000, a record. That works out to roughly one of every 900 Americans.

Thus, at the very time that some 2.5 million Americans were sinking below the government's poverty line, perennially being adjusted upward to allow for rising prices, another 240,000 Americans were comfortably within the millionaire ranks.

Other figures indicate, moreover, that the ranks of the millionaires have been swelling far more rapidly than can be explained simply by inflation. As recently as 1962, there were a relatively few 67,000 millionaires in the U.S. Inflation alone could not possibly account for all of the subsequent increase to 240,000. The explanation also lies in a little-recognized aspect of inflation. It is that keeping ahead of the price spiral is generally easier for the very rich. There are several reasons for this.

The very rich are in a position to buy the best legal and financial advice. And keeping ahead of inflation requires the most astute sort of tax and investment strategies. Let us suppose, for example, that during a given year the CPI climbs seven percent. High-income individuals would far likelier have investments yielding more than seven percent than middle-income or poor people. Indeed, in some recent years of severe inflation the average rate paid on standard bank savings accounts has been closer to five percent than seven percent. Moreover, such accounts normally are fully taxable. Yet, such accounts are precisely the sort of place where the middle class and poor tend to deposit whatever they manage to save.

The wealthy, on the other hand, are able to put money into investments that yield far more and yet often are subject to little or no taxation. A rich New Yorker, for example, in recent years has been able to obtain tax-free yields of eight percent and more by buying New York City and New York State securities. Not only do such purchases require some expertise in procedure, but a reasonably large minimum denomination is generally necessary. Often, relatively high-yielding securities may only be bought in denominations of $1,000 or even $5,000. The friendly savings bank around the corner has no such restrictions. Moreover, buying such securities can be arduous. It frequently entails the help of an intermediary, such as a securities broker, or in the case of some governmental securities a trip to one of a dozen regional Federal Reserve Banks scattered around the country.

In this connection, it is interesting to observe that investing in short-term federal government securities—primarily Treasury bills—afforded the best protection against the soaring inflation and plunging stock market of 1973-74. The small investor whose savings sat, fully taxable, in a local bank or, worse, eroded in the stock market still bears deep financial scars. But the savvy fellow who kept reinvesting in Treasury bills—rolling them over in the Wall Street jargon—survived remarkably well. The return on such securities approached double-digit levels during that period. In addition, because they are federally issued, their yield is exempt from state and local taxation. For a resident of, say, New York, where such taxes loom large indeed, this exemption constitutes a most important investment consideration.

Still more sophisticated investment strategies help the wealthy to fare far better in inflationary times than the rest of the population. For example, investors who bought South African gold-mining stocks in the early 1970's managed to keep well ahead of inflation as the prices of such shares soared. However, such investments are hardly of the sort that would occur to most individuals. Simply to purchase such securities entails a considerable familiarity with such esoteric matters as "American Depository Receipts" and the payment of South African as well as U.S. taxes. Because such stocks are highly volatile, such investments also demand almost constant watching. This is no easy task, for only a few newspapers even carry share prices of South African securities. After soaring in the early 1970's, and in the process providing superb protection against inflation, these securities plunged. Investors who weren't nimble when the turnabout came soon saw their investment profits melt away.

The performance of South African gold-mining stocks during the early 1970's is only one illustration of how sophisticated, well-informed, wealthy investors are far better qualified to protect their assets against the corrosive effect of inflation than the rest of the population. Other relatively esoteric investment techniques, mainly available to the rich, range from commodity trading to various tax-shelter arrangements still offered despite legislative efforts in Washington to reduce their attractiveness. These range from oil deals to pig-farming to movie-financing.

Altogether, it is clear that inflation tends to widen rather than diminish inequality of wealth within the population. The rich, through their sophistication in investment affairs, generally manage to uncover strategies that protect the purchasing power of their assets from being eroded severely, or at all, by rising prices. The poor and the middle class, particularly those not represented by labor unions, are not so fortunate. Ultimately, the gap between the very rich and the rest of the citizenry widens.

* * *

One should note, parenthetically, that over the years the Democratic Party has tended to pursue the sorts of economic policies most likely to generate inflation. Traditionally, the Democrats have been readier than the Republicans to accept a substantial degree of inflation as a price that must be paid to try to hold down joblessness and open up more jobs. The Democrats in general have tended to be less alarmed than the Republicans by huge federal budget deficits. They also have tended, unlike their Republican counterparts, to urge Federal Reserve officials to promote relatively rapid, inflation-producing rates of growth in the nation's money supply.

The upshot is ironic indeed. The Democrats, to the extent that their economic policies have quickened the economic pace—and the inflationary pace—have acted also to widen the gulf between groups of Americans. The conventional wisdom, of course, is that the Republicans are the rich man's party. But a close scrutiny of the facts suggests that in truth it is the Democratic Party whose policies over the decades have most benefited the rich.

* * *

The insidious impact of inflation on large segments of the country's population can be glimpsed in many ways. It can be glimpsed, for example, within the ranks of organized labor. While inflation, as we have noted, tends to widen the financial gap between the rich and other Americans, it also acts to widen the gap between different groups of American workers.

This can be detected in statistics compiled by the Bureau of Labor Statistics. They show, as one analyst of labor-force developments has put it, that inflation has "sharpened the line" between the haves and have-nots within the country's labor force.

In a recent 36-month period, the consumer-price index rose approximately 28 percent. In that same interval, other figures show earnings of workers in the largest, most powerful unions climbed appreciably faster than inflation, while earnings of workers in comparatively weak, poorly organized occupations increased more slowly than the overall price rise. In the period, for example, earnings of coal miners rose about 47 percent, refinery workers 41 percent, autoworkers 35 percent, and steelworkers 31 percent. In contrast, earnings of laundry workers increased 26 percent, hotel workers 22 percent, textile workers 22 percent, and apparel-store employees only 18 percent.

Clearly, workers in these sorts of jobs suffered a contraction of pay during the 36 months, if the totals are adjusted to allow for the 28 percent jump in the consumer price index. At the same time, however, workers in big, powerful industrial unions—autos, steel, coal and so on—mustered sufficient bargaining-table clout to increase the purchasing power of their paychecks. The dichotomy within the ranks of labor illustrates a nasty aspect of inflation—the powerful, whether investors or labor unions, often manage to keep ahead of spiraling prices, while others helplessly must see their resources erode.

* * *

The impact of inflation on the weekly paycheck of an American worker with a wife and two children can be seen in a statistical series compiled by the BLS. It takes the average weekly pay of such a worker and adjusts the total to remove federal tax and Social Security payments and the effects of inflation on purchasing power. The resulting figure can be said to represent reasonably accurately the actual buying power of such a worker's weekly paycheck. The purchasing-power figure, in the view of many analysts, provides a way of gauging the rise or fall of a typical American family's standard of living.

The BLS records make clear that, in large part on account of inflation, the typical family's paycheck buying power has been shrinking. In a recent 12-year span, for example, weekly purchasing power declined about $1. In a recent two-year interval, a time of particularly harsh price increases, weekly purchasing power fell nearly $10.

This dismal performance contrasts with the trend of purchasing power in earlier post-World War II years, before the mid-1960's, when price increases in most years were relatively moderate or prices did not rise at all but declined. Between 1958 and 1964, for instance, the weekly purchasing-power figure jumped about $10. Interestingly, weekly purchasing power has often fallen during years deemed periods of economic expansion and risen during alleged recessionary periods. Examples of the former phenomenon include 1956, 1966 and 1973. Conversely, paycheck purchasing power rose during the 1953-54 recession and in the 1960-61 recession. The explanation for this paradox is simply that inflation tended to more than offset pay gains during many supposedly good business years, while flat or declining price levels tended to ease greatly or erase the recessionary pay squeeze. Of course, the BLS statistic does not take into account the extent to which joblessness tends to climb during recessions or diminish in times of economic expansion. Altogether, however, the record leaves no doubt that, because of inflation, seemingly huge pay gains during the past couple of decades have proved meaningless. The average worker's purchasing power has stagnated, clearly unable to get ahead of spiraling prices.

The ways in which inflation has eroded purchasing power can be pinpointed across a wide range of products. In a recent decade, according to government data, the average price of a new one-family home soared 98 percent. Other increases during the same span include the price of a loaf of bread, up 52 percent; a one-pound hamburger, up 59 percent; a new car, up 95 percent; a gallon of gasoline, up 85 percent; a visit to the doctor, up 107 percent; a pack a cigarettes, up 71 percent; a man's suit, up 40 percent; a ticket to the movies, up 86 percent; the legal cost of drafting a simple will, up 110 percent; the cost of a year at a private college, up 110 percent.

* * *

Besides eroding the living standard of a typical American worker and his family, inflation is affecting U.S. family life in another adverse way. Noted earlier was the fact that more and more wives are entering the labor force nowadays. This trend partly reflects such diverse developments as the women's-liberation movement and the increasing use of labor-saving appliances and other devices in homes. But it also appears to reflect, in all too many instances, the hard economic fact that inflation is driving up family bills to a point where a second family breadwinner becomes necessary simply for the household's economic survival. Indeed, a study by the AFL-CIO finds that most housewives, indeed most women, work because of financial need. Discussing the findings of the survey, Anne Draper, an AFL-CIO economist, declares: "In general, the lower the husband's income, the greater the likelihood that the wife was working." She refutes any idea that "a woman's decision to work or not work is largely voluntary."

Many factors doubtless are involved, but it surely is more than coincidental that the exodus of housewives from the home to the office or factory comes at a time of soaring divorce rates, soaring juvenile crime and unprecedented drug use and mental illness among the young. The link between such social problems and the relentless economic problem of inflation appears a good deal closer than many sociologists might suspect.

* * *

Social progress, of course, hinges on economic progress to a considerable degree. Rapid economic growth can lead to assorted benefits in areas not directly tied to business affairs. For example, prosperous business activities mean increased tax revenues for federal, state and local levels of government. To the extent that the tax revenues are wisely used, social benefits will presumably result. By the same token, prosperous corporations and prosperous individual investors have long been a major force in the growth of tax-free foundations in the U.S. Such foundations, of course, also constitute a major factor in efforts to promote social well-being across America.

However, evidence has been piling up in recent years to suggest that inflation retards, rather than fosters, economic growth and prosperity. Increasingly, analysts have come to view inflation as a harbinger, ultimately, of bad rather than good economic times. Inflation does indeed tend to slow the economy's growth, experience indicates. The reasons are not difficult to ascertain.

For one thing, a distinct, close relationship exists between the rate at which prices happen to be rising and the interest that lenders charge on loans. Obviously, no one wants to be repaid a loan over the years in vastly cheaper dollars, unless the currency depreciation is more than offset by hefty interest charges. Accordingly, if the economic outlook seems likely to contain severe, perhaps accelerating inflation far into the future, interest rates, particularly on long-term loans, will doubtless be lofty. And high interest rates tend to restrict economic growth. For instance, they serve to inhibit corporate executives from undertaking long-term projects to expand and modernize production facilities. Unless a corporation is extraordinarily rich in cash, new plant projects normally are financed through loans, often in the form of corporate bond issues. If interest rates are high, therefore, this will tend to discourage at least some plant projects.

If facilities are not modernized, and if new facilities utilizing more efficient production techniques are not built, economic growth will tend to slow. Factory operations will be costlier and less competitive in the world marketplace. Gains in worker productivity will come harder if aging equipment is not replaced. Pay gains will become more difficult to offset through rising productivity. Per-unit labor costs, and ultimately prices, will eventually climb. Individual paychecks may soar, but the purchasing power of these paychecks, as we have seen, will rise more slowly or even decline. Ultimately, "real" economic expansion—business gains stripped of dollar "growth" that reflects merely rising prices—will tend to stagnate.

In sum, inflation acts to restrict economic growth. Besides its impact on interest rates and plant projects, it also inhibits economic expansion through its effect on consumer attitudes. Consumer spending accounts for roughly two-thirds of overall economic activity in the U.S. It is the most important element within the broad business spectrum. Logically, one would expect that consumers, fearing severe inflation ahead, would dash out to buy everything from nuts to bolts before the prices climb. However, experience shows that, in the U.S. at least, this has not been the general reaction.

Inflation has tended, for example, to inhibit one huge consumer-spending area—housing expenditures—in much the same manner that it has inhibited business outlays. To the extent that interest rates climb, mortgage loans grow costlier and home-building and home-buying is deterred. But the impact of an inflationary outlook on consumer outlays extends far beyond simply the housing industry.

"Consumers typically react defensively to rising inflation," says Gary M. Wenglowski, economist at Goldman, Sachs & Co., a large New York-based securities concern. "High rates of inflation have usually been accompanied by relatively high rates of saving; conversely, the low inflation rates of the mid 1950's and early 1960's were associated with relatively low saving rates."

A close relationship between the desire to save and the fear of inflation—however illogical that may seem—can be glimpsed in a few statistics. In 1946, consumers saved 9.6 percent of their after-tax earnings—and the consumer-price index rose 8.5 percent, an increase that makes even recent price jumps seem not all that bad. In 1951, similarly, the saving rate averaged 7.6 percent—and consumer prices climbed 7.9 percent. In 1955, on the other hand, savings came to only 5.7 percent of after-tax earnings—and consumer prices actually declined slightly. And in 1963, the saving rate stood at 4.9 percent—and the consumer-price index rose only 1.2 percent.

Another reason for high savings during periods of high inflation, Mr. Wenglowski claims, "is the lofty level of interest rates that normally accompanies inflation; a sharp enough rise in interest rates can both discourage consumer borrowing and encourage consumer saving." An analyst at New York's Chase Manhattan Bank adds this comment: "People save because they fear inflation, but in the process they eventually begin to defeat inflation, and so wind up saving less." In a similar vein, Henry Wallich, a former professor of economics at Yale University and a governor of the Federal Reserve Board, likes to startle his friends with the statement that "inflation, as far as the consumer is concerned, is deflationary." The reluctance of consumers to spend when prices begin to rise rapidly has been insufficient in recent years to stop inflation dead in its tracks. There is evidence, however, that the seemingly illogical reaction of consumers to accelerating price increases has made recent inflation somewhat less severe than it might otherwise have been.

* * *

One of the most serious inequities caused by spiraling prices involves the relationship between the progressive income tax and inflation. Henry Hazlitt, the economist, discussing the effect of this tax on American breadwinners, observes that the price spiral "keeps pushing them into higher tax brackets; they are called upon to pay higher percentage rates even though their real income may not have gone up at all." In addition, he notes, "many are forced to pay taxes on so-called capital gains when in real terms they may actually have suffered capital losses."

Not surprisingly, inflation tends to sap incentive, particularly among individuals who find their purchasing power eroding even as their pay reaches higher and higher income brackets. As incentive diminishes, so often does hard work. Eventually, as we have seen, productivity gains diminish as well.

Inflation leads to sloppy budget-keeping in Washington as well as in the home. Only in a time of rampant inflation would it be possible for federal budget administrators to "lose" billions of dollars. Michael E. Levy, a senior economist at the Conference Board in New York, estimates that during the second quarter of 1976, for example, the federal government authorized some $9 billion for spending programs that somehow was not spent. "About half the lost outlays of the second quarter cannot be fully traced" because of insufficient record-keeping, the analyst says, adding that the other half also cannot be fully accounted for. Loose accounting practices and inflation, it appears, go hand in hand.

Inflation and crime are also bedfellows, experience indicates. There is no question that tax cheating has proliferated in recent years. Some analysts believe that an actual taxpayer revolt in the U. S. is possible in the years just ahead, as inflation keeps pushing more and more workers into the top tax brackets. And it is not simply income taxes that are stirring taxpayer antagonism. A study made in areas near Washington, D.C., for instance, finds that property taxes paid on single-family houses soared nearly 225 percent during a recent decade. Property-tax revenues across the country have recently been climbing at an annual rate of more than 10 percent.

Much tax cheating goes undetected. Recorded crime of all sorts, at the same time, is costing the nation "at least $125 billion," according to a report by the Joint Economic Committee of Congress. A precise estimate is impossible, but authorities are convinced that the total, a record each year, is continuing to rise at a rapid pace.

* * *

Perhaps the clearest illustration of inflation's dark side is provided by the horrendous German encounter with soaring prices in the early 1920's.

Even in today's inflationary economic environment, the raw statistics of Germany's inflation make awesome reading. In August 1922, Germany's money supply totaled 252 billion marks. In January 1923, it was 2 trillion. In September 1923, it stood at 28 quadrillion and in November 1923, it reached 497 quintillion—or the number 497 followed by no less than 18 zeroes.

This runaway inflation of the German money supply ended, finally, when the currency became virtually worthless, its stated value worth less than the cost of the paper it was printed upon. The old mark was replaced in 1924 by a new Reichsmark whose value was set at 1 billion old marks. The old marks were withdrawn from circulation and ceased to be legal tender.

In late 1923, near the final collapse of the German currency, some corporations took to reimbursing their employees with special scrip that could be used to buy company products. Borrowing became nearly impossible. All sorts of goods were in short supply. Food riots erupted in cities. Prices changed by the hour.

Obviously, there could be no precise record kept of the price spiral in those desperate months. But a book by Frank D. Graham, an American economist, titled *Exchange, Prices and Production in Hyper-Inflation: Germany, 1920-1923*, does trace the country's wholesale-price index through December 1922. At the start of that year, the index stood at 4,626 times its 1913 average. By December 1922, it reached 374,563,426,600 times the 1913 average.

Statistics bearing on other facets of the German price spiral are available through the entire period. Employment, perhaps surprisingly, held up quite well until just before the currency collapsed. As late as July 1923, only 3.5 percent of Germany's trade-union members were without jobs. This actually was lower than the rate of 6 percent in July 1920, three years earlier, when prices were just starting to soar. As things got out of hand near the end of 1923, however, joblessness climbed sharply. The jobless rate went from 3.5 percent in July to 9.9 percent in September to a ghastly 28.2 percent in December. The last rate exceeds the highest rate recorded during the pit of the Great Depression in the United States during the 1930's.

Mr. Graham discusses why employment, as well as economic activity generally, remained at a high level until near the end: "The more rapid the rise in prices, the greater became the intensity of demand. Business boomed, unemployment vanished, sales were all too easy. There was of course an enormous amount of buying which, under other circumstances, would have been quite senseless. People purchased not what they wanted to use but whatever they could get. . . . One could produce anything material and be sure of a market."

An index measuring the volume of the country's physical output of goods, contained in the Graham book, underscores this rising demand, before the collapse, for "anything material." The index stood at 61 percent of the 1913 average in 1920, rose to 77 percent in 1921 and then climbed to 86 percent in 1922. A year later, however, it was down to 54 percent. As late as 1927, the index was still at the 1922 level.

The inflation's impact on savings also has been noted. Depositors who left their funds in savings banks throughout the period lost everything. In 1913, some 19 billion marks were on deposit in savings banks. In November 1924, that sum had the purchasing power of one-quarter of an American penny. The rush to take savings out of the bank as inflation worsened forced many thrift institutions to close their doors. In 1913 there were 10,890 savings-bank offices in the country. By 1924, there were only 4,870.

The story was much the same in the insurance business. In 1913 there were some 16 million life insurance policies outstanding. By 1924, the total was barely 3 million. At the worst of the price spiral the postage stamp on an envelope containing an insurance payment to a beneficiary often cost more than the sum written on the enclosed check.

Those months weren't a happy time for stock-market investors either. A share-price index was recorded by another economic historian, Costantino Bresciani-Turroni, an Italian professor. This index has been adjusted to express values in dollar terms. It stood at 49.68 at the start of 1919. By February 1920, it was down to 8.47. Then as business activity became more frantic, it began to climb, reaching 26.80 by the end of 1922. The climb continued through much of 1923, but share prices plunged again near the end of the year, when economic chaos set in. A study cited by Mr. Bresciani-Turroni found that an investor who had bought a typical group of stocks in 1914 would, by 1924, have retained only one-quarter of his original investment, expressed in terms of gold. By then, company bankruptcies, which had been rare during the booming years, were widespread.

Another victim of the price spiral in Germany during the

early 1920's was efficiency. The Bresciani-Turroni book recalls that in a typical large production company there were 120 "unproductive" employees for every 100 actual production-line workers in 1922. This compared with 66 for every 100 in 1913. One reason was that more and more office personnel were required to handle rapidly changing price lists, more frequent cost-of-living pay supplements, incessant disputes with labor unions, increasingly complex tax and accounting problems and spreading supply and production bottlenecks.

A wide range of other economic phenomena occurred. Exports rose briskly in the early inflation years, as the mark got cheaper on foreign exchange markets. But near the end, export volume sagged as shortages developed. Various export controls were imposed to try to prevent still worse shortages. At the same time, the quality of workmanship deteriorated. An index of quality for various products, published in a German newspaper, dropped from a level of 1.00 in April 1921 to 0.82 in October 1922 to 0.64 in October 1923. After the currency collapse, it began to move up again, reaching 1.24 in April 1924, a time of depressed business activity.

Other trends evident at that time included a tendency toward greater economic concentration. Larger companies gobbled up smaller companies. Fearing shortages, companies that produced, for example, consumer goods sought mergers with companies that supplied them with raw materials. On an individual level, inflation led to a greater concentration of wealth among the rich. Investors with sufficient financial sophistication to foresee the worsening price spiral were able to hedge much more effectively against it than the middle class, the poor or older persons on fixed incomes.

Crime rose rapidly during the years of the German inflation. An index reflecting the total number of crimes committed stood at 136 percent of the 1882 average in 1921. By 1923, it was 170 percent. After the price spiral ended, however, it fell sharply, to 150 percent in 1924 and to 122 percent in 1925. Crimes committed by young men, particularly, paralleled price developments. Such crimes soared to 212 percent of the 1882 average in 1923 and then fell to 153 percent in 1924 and to 87 percent in 1925.

Other sociological ramifications of Germany's inflation years are less easily pinpointed. It's widely held, however, that the country's increasing prejudice against Jews and the subsequent rise of Adolf Hitler can be traced to that time. Perhaps the most puzzling aspect of the period was the willingness of German leaders to continue along the inflationary path for so long once the hazards had become clear.

Professor Bresciani-Turroni concluded that the authorities simply lacked "the courage to resist the pressure of those who demanded ever greater quantities of paper money, and to face boldly" the temporary business setback that would no doubt have followed a prompter return to more conservative monetary policies. In the economist's view, this lack of courage to curb a developing boom through stricter policies, rather than the burden of World War I debts, was "the fundamental cause of the depreciation of the mark" and all the economic and sociological problems that went with it.

Clearly, the German experience of the early 1920's holds vital lessons for Americans in the current inflationary time, which, fortunately, has not yet reached anything like the frenetic levels that existed in the Germany of those days.

CHAPTER SEVEN

Inflation's Engine

A. Gary Shilling, a prominent private economic forecaster in New York, has studied the nature of inflation over many decades. As an economic forecaster, he has been remarkably accurate in predicting general price behavior. Discussing his forecasting technique, he explains, quite simply, that inflation "can't have a life of its own." The forecaster's task, he goes on, is to discern whether underlying forces that can produce inflation exist within the economy at a particular time, or appear likely to develop.

Forces that produce inflation, that combine to constitute what economists occasionally call inflation's engine, are diverse. However, as Gary Shilling indicates, they can with some effort be identified and assessed.

Very generally, these forces can be segregated into three categories—excessive spending, invariably well-intentioned, within governmental sectors of the economy; sharply climbing costs that all too often seem to defy reasonable control; and excessive production and use of money in all its forms.

* * *

Let us glance first at the governmental role in inflation. A study by New York's Conference Board provides, as an introduction, an outline of the growth of government in the U.S. Employment at all levels of government—federal, state and local—more than doubled in a recent 20-year period, the study states. In the span, public-sector employment rose to 15 million persons from 7.4 million. State and local governments, which employ more than 12 million workers, accounted for most of the increase. Federal civilian jobs—this may surprise many readers—actually declined during some of the 20 years, particularly during the late 1960's and early 1970's.

Altogether, according to the report, 19.2 percent of all nonfarm workers are employed by some level of government, up from 13.3 percent in 1950. These individuals receive a combined payroll of more than $13 billion a month, or five times the comparable payment two decades ago.

Over the 20-year period, federal civilian workers expanded their ranks by a minuscule one-tenth of one percent. But their payroll expanded 8 percent.

Huge increases in the ranks of persons employed by state and local government agencies during the 20 years are reported in the study. Local government employees swelled from just under four million to about nine million, a rise of more than 100 percent. State government workers proliferated still more sharply, from about one million to nearly 3.5 million, a gain of more than 200 percent. The monthly payroll costs of local government employees surged from roughly $1 billion to about $7.5 billion in the period. State-employee payroll costs soared from $300 million monthly to about $2.7 billion monthly.

"A major reason for the rise in state and local employment

and payrolls is that the task of providing most civilian services falls upon these governments," the Conference Board analysis declares. "To meet demands for better and more sophisticated services in social programs—and the improved quality of life these imply—expansion and increased spending have occurred."

Of course, payroll costs are by no means the only expenditures involved. In only 10 years, between 1965 and 1975, overall expenditures by state and local governments surged from $101 billion to $318.5 billion. These agencies' purchases of goods and services accounted for $215 billion in 1975, more than 14 percent of America's gross national product for that year. By comparison, the 1965 figure of $101 billion represents less than 8 percent of 1965's GNP figure.

Reviewing such statistics the Conference Board study notes: "Direct spending by state and local Governments swelled most rapidly for education, health and hospitals, and public welfare. This increase was related to the changing age mix in the U.S. population as well as an extension and upgrading of services and technology. Demands centered around the needs for baby-boom children, who had reached school age during a trend toward longer education, and the growing numbers of the aged, more prone to illness and poverty."

Greater governmental spending, to be sure, meant more taxes. State collections rose from $26 billion in 1965 to $80 billion in 1975. Local taxes increased over the same period from $25 billion to $61 billion. Sales and general-revenue taxes contributed the most to the coffers of the states, according to the study, while property taxes were the prime source of income for local Governments.

The Conference Board report also breaks down the precise

growth pattern of spending by state and local authorities during 1965-75. The sharpest increase is accounted for by welfare outlays, up 331 percent in the period. Next among the major categories is interest on outstanding debt, up 253 percent. Then comes health-and-hospitals spending, up 251 percent. Other huge gains during the decade include sanitation expenditures, up 212 percent; education spending, up 208 percent; police and fire protection, up 207 percent; financial administration outlays, up 184 percent; spending on recreational and natural resources, up 171 percent. The only major category showing an increase of less than 150 percent in the 10 years is a surprise—highway expenditures. Even this relative laggard, however, registered an 84 percent rise.

In absolute terms, educational outlays, at $88 billion, bulked larger than any other single category in 1975. Welfare expenditures, leading in terms of percentage gain over the period, amounted to nearly $28 billion in 1975, far behind the total spent on education. About $23 billion was spent during the year on highways and $19 billion on health and hospitals. Some $12 billion was accounted for by police and fire expenditures. No other major spending category topped $10 billion, according to the report.

In all, the picture that emerges from such data is clear. We have witnessed a vast, steep increase in governmental outlays, not at the closely watched, much-publicized federal level, but at the state and local levels—city hall, state house, the local school district, the county office. Such governmental spending has increased dramatically and now looms large indeed across the country's economic landscape.

And, of course, federal outlays must not be disregarded. It's true that federal outlays have shown less growth. But the expenditures remain enormous, and there are solid grounds to suppose that this spending will be briskly on the rise in the years just ahead.

* * *

Arthur F. Burns, the former Federal Reserve Board chairman, stresses the role of governmental overspending as a major force behind today's inflation. Indeed, he believes that "the main source of inflation is the tendency of modern governments to expand their outlays at a rapid rate in response to incessant demands from the electorate." The veteran economist maintains that "governments nowadays try to solve almost every economic and social ill by spending money."

Regarding the U.S., Mr. Burns remarks: "With expenditures increasing faster than revenues, our own government has persistently been paying out a great deal more to the public than it takes in from the public by way of taxes." In a recent 10 years, he recalls, "the accumulated deficit [in the federal budget] comes to something like $220 billion." He adds that if one also considers other federal outlays not directly covered in the federal budget, such as the spending of certain federal agencies—"as I think you should"—then the accumulated deficit "comes to about $300 billion" over the 10 years. Such overspending, he asserts, "has been the main cause of our inflation since the mid-1960's."

* * *

Figures compiled by the U.S. Office of Management and Budget, or OMB, trace the federal spending rise over the past quarter-century. As recently as 1955, such spending amounted to just under $71 billion. A decade later, in 1965, it was edging over the $100 billion mark. Since then, the rise has sharply accelerated—to above $250 billion in 1974 and, as the climb has steepened, to above $500 billion recently. That amounts to more than seven times the 1955 total.

Let us glance briefly at some of the places that this federal money goes. Social-welfare programs rank high on the list. Until about 1965, state and local governments provided most of the money for social-welfare programs. But in recent years the situation has changed so that the bulk of such money—over 60 percent—now comes from Washington. Such programs in a recent six-year interval swelled from $146 billion to about $332 billion, an increase of more than 125 percent. The sharpest gain occurred in governmental outlays for welfare housing—up 343 percent during the period, from $700 million to $3.1 billion. In absolute terms, the largest gain took place within the vast "social insurance" category covering mainly retirement benefits. This expanded from $54.7 billion to $146.6 billion during the half-dozen years.

Health spending rose in the period from $13.1 billion to $33.4 billion. Analysts generally agree that the government's role in providing health care for the citizenry will inevitably expand, so that this particular element of federal spending is likely, if anything, to rise even more rapidly in coming years.

The branch of the federal government directly in charge of most of this vast spending is the Department of Health, Education and Welfare. HEW, as the department is called, grew in a recent 24-year period from an organization staffed by 37,000 bureaucrats to one employing more than 157,000. In 1977, the department administered 381 statutory programs ranging from Social Security to welfare payments for the blind. Under its auspicies are the National Institutes of Health in Washington, the Center for Disease Control in

Atlanta and the Food and Drug Administration, a longtime champion of consumer protection at the supermarket and the pharmacy.

One means of gauging HEW's vastly enlarged role is to compare its outlays with those of the Department of Defense. The latter, of course, has been much criticized over the years as an overspender and prime culprit in the country's inflationary trouble. It is true that military spending tends to exert a particularly inflationary impact. This is because defense outlays normally do nothing to increase the country's supply of goods and services that people can buy and use. Yet, defense spending obviously pours millions into the pockets of workers who collect paychecks for military jobs. There occurs a vast expansion of consumer buying power without any concurrent increase in the available supply of things to purchase. The upshot is an intensification of inflationary pressure within the economy.

Be that as it may, the fact remains that outlays administered by HEW surpassed those overseen by the Defense Department in 1972. In 1953, HEW's initial year, its expenditures were $1.9 billion, while the Defense Department total amounted to $47.5 billion. Since the two lines crossed in 1972, at roughly the $80 billion mark, HEW outlays have increasingly outdistanced the Defense figures. An estimate for 1978 places the HEW total at about $170 billion and Defense expenditures at about $111 billion. It is difficult to imagine that precisely 25 years earlier, the Defense level was nearly 25 times higher than that of HEW.

* * *

As governmental outlays have risen and caused inflationary pressures to build within the economy, it is no coincidence that costs of countless items have also tended to increase sharply, aggravating the price spiral.

In a recent four years, for example, the average cost to American consumers of electricity has soared more than 50 percent. Other cost increases during the period include gas for heating, up 70 percent; meats, up 40 percent; clothing, up 25 percent; medical care, up 45 percent; household appliances, up 20 percent; new cars, up 28 percent; dairy products, up 50 percent.

A huge cost that has been sharply on the rise in recent years is the expense of labor. The labor-cost spiral requires special attention. Pay, whether hourly or weekly, whether defined to include sundry fringe benefits or limited to the sum of all weekly paychecks, has been steeply rising for more than a decade. This big increase, however, would not be a major inflationary force within the economy if—and this is a key consideration—if worker productivity had managed over the years to advance apace or faster.

The example of a worker in a widget factory comes to mind. He receives a 10 percent raise in his hourly pay. But his hourly production of widgets also increases 10 percent. And so the employer's labor costs per widget produced remain unchanged. The upshot is that the employer comes under no new pressure to raise his prices and protect his profit margin as a result of the 10 percent pay boost. For many years after World War II, this is precisely what transpired. Pay increased year after year. But productivity—hourly per-worker output of widgets or whatever—increased approximately as rapidly as pay. In some years, the pay gains slightly exceeded the productivity advance. In other years, productivity rose slightly faster than pay. In the end, year after year, per-unit labor costs remained about flat. And, as a result, one potential source of inflationary pressure remained dormant.

In recent years, as unions have become more demanding, pay increases have repeatedly exceeded productivity gains. The widget worker now gets a 15 percent pay boost while his productivity increases only 5 percent. The per-widget cost of his labor, in such circumstances, soars 10 percent, and the widget company comes under intense pressure to raise its prices in order to offset climbing unit labor costs and protect its profit margin.

Some companies have managed to impose higher and higher prices to offset their climbing labor costs. This pattern has contributed to the overall price spiral of recent years. Other companies have been less fortunate. Most have attempted to impose higher prices. But many whose products are less than essential have seen their markets shrink sharply as prices have been put up. Some have lost ground to competing, substitute products, others to similar products made in countries where labor has remained relatively cheap.

The sad irony is that, as U.S. labor costs outstrip productivity gains, the inflation that results ultimately hurts, among others, the very workers who receive the big pay boosts. Government statistics show that, in a recent decade marked by huge pay increases and relatively meager productivity gains, the actual buying power of most Americans' paychecks failed to grow at all. The inflation, caused in part by climbing labor costs, served to wipe out any improvement in the all-important area of purchasing power. What good is a 20 percent pay increase if prices, as a result, jump 21 percent?

A few statistics drive home the futility of today's labor-cost spiral. Unit labor costs in the nation's manufacturing industries soared some 70 percent in a recent 10-year period. In other words, labor costs—even after taking offsetting productivity gains into account—surged. By comparison, the same labor-cost measure remained approximately flat between 1955 and 1965.

Other governmental data show that, in the same 10 years of soaring labor costs, the purchasing power of the average weekly paycheck barely budged. Expressed in terms of the 1967 price level, it hovered around $90. By comparison, the same paycheck purchasing-power measure climbed about $10, or roughly 12 percent, during the 1955-65 span.

If productivity gains could somehow be vastly enlarged, the labor-cost spiral of recent years, to a considerable extent, could be brought under control. In the process, purchasing power would benefit to the extent that inflation tended to ease. However, productivity gains come hard. They depend on the energy, enthusiasm and skill of employees. But they also depend on the caliber of equipment supplied to the work force. The aforementioned widget worker who produces 10 percent more widgets each hour in all probability does so mainly because of some improvement in his widget-making facilities. Perhaps his employer has provided him with a new widget-gadget that hops, skips and jumps more briskly than the old widget-gadget. Or perhaps this year's widget has been redesigned in such a way that widget-making now requires only 22 steps instead of 35 steps.

When newspaper headlines report that productivity in a recent quarter rose, say, at an annual rate of three percent—beware. The chances are that some new widget-making machines have come into operation, or that old ones are somehow being used more efficiently. It is almost surely not simply a case of more enthusiastic, more energetic work habits.

* * *

Accordingly, a major key to larger and larger productivity advances each year is the ability of American employers to maintain facilities that are as up-to-date and efficient as possible. And here, unhappily, the record is less than enviable. For a variety of reasons, American corporations have been slow to modernize their facilities. The American steel industry, once the envy of steelmakers around the world, has recently fallen so far behind Japan's, in terms of modernizing, that it has been compelled to seek out Japanese expertise in planning new facilities in the U.S. Chicago-based Inland Steel Company, for instance, recently held up plans to install a new oxygen-furnace facility, pending discussions with Japanese oxygen-furnace experts.

One reason for this sort of backsliding involves U.S. tax laws. While precise regulations in America have recently been changing almost as frequently as seats in the Congress, the overriding fact is that U.S. regulations in general provide employers with less tax incentive to repair and modernize their facilities than the rules provide in Japan or in much of Western Europe.

Another problem, less simple to correct than out-of-date tax laws, involves American efforts to clean up—and keep clean—the environment.

There can be little question about the need to curb production facilities that befoul the nation's air, water and soil. And there can be little question that America has made a solid start toward this end. A decade ago, the Buffalo River in New York State was so befouled by industrial waste that it literally caught fire. Today, in magnificent contrast, game fish are returning to the river.

Notwithstanding such recent strides, much remains to be done and the effort must be a continuing one, decade after decade. The government-sponsored Council on Environmental Quality has drawn up the bill for cleaning up America, an estimate of pollution-control costs over the next decade. The various costs are expressed in terms of the 1976 price level, so that with continuing inflation the actual expense in so-called current dollars—the kind residing in your wallet or purse—will be much, much higher.

The study views air pollution as the number one problem. It puts the air clean-up bill at $143 billion. This breaks down as follows:

Auto-caused air pollution, $56 billion, to be footed largely by auto companies; factory-caused air pollution, $49 billion, to be paid mainly by the particular private companies involved; air pollution caused by power-generating stations, $32 billion, to be financed by the utilities responsible; air pollution from public buildings, incinerators and other government-run facilities, $6 billion, to be paid by the government.

The study places the water-pollution bill, totaling $116 billion, a close second to the air-pollution bill. The breakdown follows:

Water pollution caused by factories, $59 billion, to be provided by the companies involved; utilities-caused water pollution, $13 billion, to be paid by the power companies responsible; pollution caused by waste-treatment plants and sewers, $44 billion, to be financed by the governmental agency involved.

The study also estimates that another $8 billion will be needed in the decade to fight pollution caused by solid wastes and radiation, and another $4 billion to combat noise pollution.

In all, the pollution fight totals $271 billion. This is a huge expense—especially when one recalls that the amount is stated in terms of 1976 prices. Yet it is a cost that most responsible observers feel is unavoidable. And, as such, it looms large in any attempt to assess the forces of inflation that continue to plague the American economy. Not only is the clean-up bill immense, but the emphasis on pollution-fighting is bound to complicate productivity gains in the years ahead.

* * *

Let us return briefly to the business of making widgets. The widget-maker's boss does indeed strongly desire to speed up productivity at the factory. And to do so he intends to spend one million dollars on a brand-new widget-gadget that can turn out widgets 10 percent faster than the old widget-gadget. But there are a couple of catches. The new widget-gadget, because it moves more rapidly, also spews out more smoke. So it must be fitted with a special smoke stopper that not only adds to the cost of the new machinery but necessitates a slight reduction in its rate of operation. Fitted with a smoke stopper, the new widget-gadget now turns out only 2 percent more widgets hourly—and of course the bill is higher as well.

The upshot of such a development is that the productivity gains, while they will no doubt continue to be made, may well come harder in the time ahead. Indeed, there is evidence to suggest that the slowdown has already begun. In much of the period since World War II, productivity within the U.S. economy increased at annual rates in the neighborhood of 3 percent and 4 percent. In many years—for instance, 1949, 1950, 1958 and 1961—the yearly gain was closer to 5 percent and 6 percent. But in much of the recent past, the yearly increases have been skimpier. Recently, 3 percent has represented an unusually strong yearly advance. And there have been years of late when productivity has not advanced at all but has fallen. This unfortunate tendency marked both 1973 and 1974. In the latter year, a time of recession, hourly output of workers fell nearly 2 percent. By no coincidence, unit labor costs that year soared nearly 13 percent, the sharpest such increase on record up to that time.

Some additional developments should act to make future productivity gains still more difficult. Again, the upshot is to force up unit labor costs and intensify inflation.

One of these is the likely configuration of the labor force during the years just ahead. The continuing influx of women and teen-agers into the labor force has been well publicized. The trend is undeniably welcome, to the extent that it eases frustration among housewives and young people desiring a job. But there is another side to the coin that receives scant attention. It is that productivity tends to be relatively low among those two demographic groups. Teen-agers, of course, lack experience. To the degree that experience does play some part in spurring a worker's hourly output, teen-age inexperience does generally cause somewhat reduced productivity. A smiliar lack of experience often prevails where a housewife enters the work force after years in the home.

Moreover, teen-agers and women tend to move into service-type jobs. And these jobs, ranging from barbers to newspaper reporters, generally do not lend themselves to dramatic productivity gains. How do you automate a haircut? Or the reporting of a news story? A new, faster widget machine would be of no help. In addition, service-type jobs constitute a larger and larger segment of the U.S. labor market. Indeed, for over a decade now, more than half the jobs available within the U.S. economy have been service jobs. The U.S. was the first major industrial country where service jobs exceeded the 50 percent mark. Recently, several other relatively advanced economies have followed suit. In fact, today service-type jobs bulk even larger in Sweden than in the U.S. The swing to services, most economists agree, is a natural development within relatively sophisticated economies. The irony, as we have seen, is that the trend complicates productivity advances and, ultimately, fosters inflation.

In discussions of lagging productivity and climbing labor costs, it frequently is claimed that today's American workers are, to put it bluntly, lazier than their predecessors of two or three or four decades ago. There may be some truth to this assertion, especially with today's emphasis on leisure time, but it is impossible to prove. One available yardstick, however, is a government series showing the length of the average work-week of production workers. The popular assumption is that people are working shorter and shorter hours. But the work-week statistical series, surprisingly, does not support this notion. In the past quarter-century, the work-week has remained about flat, at roughly 40 hours.

As far as working habits are concerned, a likelier drag on productivity than any innate laziness on the part of the labor force is the growing power of some large industrial unions over the work rules that companies may impose. Productivity surely suffers, to the extent that workers are prevented by regulations from performing other than rigidly defined tasks in a particular factory or wherever. It is a difficult matter to quantify. But a sampling of recent major labor contracts confirms that such restrictive regulations are proliferating. Productivity clearly is affected if, for example, the production line at our widget factory must be halted until a union-designated electrician can be called in to replace a light bulb—even if our friend the widget worker could have made the change all by himself.

* * *

No discussion of the costs underlying today's inflation would be complete without at least a glance at the drastic increase that has occurred in the cost of one key raw material—petroleum. It is no exaggeration to say that the world economy runs largely on oil. By 1980, it is estimated that world petroleum demand will approximate 55 million barrels daily. Obviously, a substantial increase in the cost of such an important raw material will have wide, significant ramifications on other costs throughout the world economy. No one can predict precisely how rapidly the cost of oil will continue to increase in coming years. One hopes that the rise will be slower than the steep climb since the early 1970's. But much clearly depends on political developments within the main oil-producing countries, particularly in the Middle East.

In this regard, a study titled *World Oil: Challenges and Opportunities* is noteworthy. Produced by economists at New York's Irving Trust Company, it states: "The conventional wisdom today is that [the oil-producing countries'] near-monopoly control of the world's oil market will last well into the 1980's, if not beyond. We challenge this point of view and suggest that a more probable outcome will be a gradual erosion of the cartel's position over the next few years. We do not foresee [the cartel] falling apart. . . . Rather, we believe that natural economic forces will gradually work toward a reassertion of market power of the oil-consuming nations."

The Irving Trust study foresees increasingly successful efforts by major oil-consuming countries, including the U.S., to conserve petroleum use and expand domestic oil output. It also envisages increasing concern within the producers' cartel that large, repeated oil-price boosts could backfire by causing a deep, worldwide recession—or worse. The study notes "the mounting international debt of many developing countries and of some industrialized nations" as oil bills climb sharply. "Chronic international payments deficits can set off a vicious devaluation-inflation cycle, which in turn brings about high unemployment or increased protectionism," the report states. On an optimistic note, Irving Trust economists anticipate that such oil-exporting giants as Saudi Arabia and Iran, with vast business investments scattered around the world, will see that excessive oil-price boosts year after year could prove self-defeating. For the moment, however, oil remains an increasingly costly item that plays a major role in the inflation plaguing a U.S. economy increasingly dependent on petroleum imports.

* * *

Another cost that keeps feeding U.S. inflation is less obvious, perhaps, than the cost of petroleum. It is the cost of taxes. They, too, tend to drive up the general price level.

Few people think of their tax bill precisely as a cost. But taxes surely are a major cost, one that has been rising steeply for many years and, barring a dramatic shift to the political right in the U.S., seems likely to keep right on climbing.

A fascinating analysis of the impact of taxes on prices was published in the mid-November 1976 issue of *Forbes Magazine*. Titled "Inflation Is Too Serious a Matter to Leave to the Economists," the article argues that the climbing cost of taxpaying, for individuals as well as businesses, has acted to drive up prices throughout the complex U.S. economy. The article challenges the view, voiced by some economists, that the country's overall tax burden has not really increased much in recent decades. "The next economist who divides the tax-take by the GNP and announces that the share of the national wealth that the federal government spends has been stable at around 20 percent for twenty years should be sued himself for malpractice," the article states. "He is forgetting state and local governments and all manner of new social legislation and social custom."

Oliver Wendell Holmes once called taxes the price that must be paid to maintain civilization. To the extent that this is so, certainly, the rising tax bill—and its inflationary ramifications—cannot be viewed as an unmitigated evil. However, Milton Friedman, the Nobel-laureate economist at the University of Chicago, has repeatedly made the point that government expenditures—of collected tax money—tend to be less efficient expenditures than money spent within the economy's private sector by individuals and businesses. The argument, quite simply, is that the profit motive, the need to watch the so-called bottom line on corporate balance sheets as well as household budgets, compels a measure of prudence not evident in Washington or at the various state capitols and city halls.

A major problem in Washington's handling of tax dollars, it should be added, is the federal government's unique position with regard to money. Unlike the private sector, unlike even the state and local levels of government, Washington can literally create money, through the Federal Reserve Board. The knowledge that more money can be produced if things get tight surely serves to subdue any inclination toward frugality.

Indeed, the importance of this money-generating capacity in Washington can hardly be understated in any discussion of inflation's underlying forces. It deserves detailed attention. As we will see in the next chapter, no ingredient of today's inflation is so important or so widely misunderstood.

CHAPTER EIGHT

The Mighty Money Machine

The proposition is strikingly simple and full of logic. Yet, it has been widely misunderstood or, worse, ignored by people in policymaking positions in the U.S. Price levels are a reflection of the relationship between money in use within the nation's economy and the supply of goods and services available to be purchased with that money.

In fundamental terms, the relationship can be readily envisaged. In the marketplace are 10 widgets available for purchase. In the marketplace, as well, are 10 customers, each supplied with $10 for widget-buying. No special mathematics is required to determine, all things being equal, that each widget will sell at $10. But now suppose that each of our 10 widget-buyers is supplied with another $5, so that each now has $15 for widget-buying. Again, it quite obviously follows that each widget will sell for $15, instead of $10.

The situation described with the widget-buyers precisely describes a basic force underlying the distressing inflation of recent years. A few statistics spell out what has been happening. Let us use the most common definition of money, which economists call M-1—defined as currency in circulation plus checking-account deposits. During a recent five-year period, M-1 increased 6.3 percent annually. During the same five years, however, the nation's output of goods and services in "real" terms—that is, adjusted for changing prices—expanded only 3.5 percent, or slightly more than half the pace of monetary expansion.

And what did prices do? Not surprisingly, the general price level jumped 5 percent annually during the period. The supply of money available for buying rose far faster than the marketplace supply of goods and services. As in the case of the widgets, prices had nowhere to go but up.

If monetary growth is extra rapid, and expansion of the supply of goods and services extra slow, experience shows that the price climb becomes especially steep. This can be seen, for example, in the recent experience of Britain, a country particularly troubled by inflation. In a recent five years, the British money supply rose 8.7 percent annually, while the supply of goods and services rose only 2.7 percent annually. The result was a 7.5 percent annual rise in British prices. To place such a rate of price increase into perspective, let us recall again the Rule of 70. Using that rule, we know that the value of the British pound will be cut in half within a decade if British prices climb only 7 percent a year. Thus, the actual 7.5 percent rate of inflation in Britain during the recent five years would halve the pound's buying power in less than a decade.

Surveying such data, Allan H. Meltzer, an economics professor at Carnegie-Mellon University in Pittsburgh, stresses that "higher average rates of monetary expansion and higher average rates of inflation are closely associated." And he goes on to note that there appears to be "no evidence that the growth of real output has increased with inflation."

* * *

In the previous chapter, we noted that the power to generate money—and an awesome power it is—resides in Washington, at the Federal Reserve Board. The Fed derives this enviable ability from the Congress, which under the U.S. Constitution (Article I, Section 8) has the authority "to coin money" and to "regulate the value thereof." The Congress, for all its virtues, is an unwieldy institution, hardly equipped to carry out the daily business of precisely regulating the size of the money supply. Accordingly, the legislators wisely delegated their constitutional money-creating power to the Fed.

Today, the Fed unit most directly involved in moneymaking is the Federal Reserve Open Market Committee. The FOMC, as the unit is called, is composed of the Federal Reserve Board's seven governors, plus five presidents of regional Federal Reserve banks. The FOMC convenes in Washington at the Federal Reserve building on Constitution Avenue, which houses the Federal Reserve Board, its seven governors and a large staff of economists and statisticians.

The Fed and the FOMC control the money supply of the country in three essential ways. The Reserve Board fixes the level of so-called reserve requirements that banks must maintain rather than lend out to customers. The higher the level of reserve requirements, the more restricted becomes bank lending. This tends to inhibit monetary growth, just as a lower level of reserve requirements tends to expand monetary growth. As money is lent by banks, deposited in other banks, lent again, and so on and so on, the checking-account component of the money supply obviously will tend to rise substantially. It is possible to determine, through mathematics, the theoretical limit of this so-called multiplier effect. The limit, clearly, will depend on where the Reserve Board sets the percentage for reserves required to be put aside. If banks are told, for instance, to keep cash reserves of 15 percent against their checking-account deposits, the theoretical limit of the multiplier effect for an original $1,000 deposit works out to $6,667. This occurs because diminishing fractions of the original $1,000 are lent and relent and relent through the banking system. The arrangement is called a "fractional-reserve" type of banking system.

The nation's money-supply level is also regulated by the Fed through the so-called discount rate. When banks need funds for lending or other uses, as members of the Federal Reserve System they may borrow from regional Federal Reserve banks. The discount rate is the interest charged by regional Fed banks on such loans. An increase in the discount rate, like a boost in reserve requirements, tends to constrict monetary growth. And a drop in the discount rate, like lower reserve requirements, tends to promote faster monetary growth.

The FOMC plays an essential role in the third, and by far the most important, way in which the Fed regulates the money supply. The FOMC meets in Washington regularly, roughly twice monthly. After dutifully studying the economic situation at the particular time, the committee decides whether the situation requires faster monetary growth, slower monetary growth, more of the same or perhaps an actual contraction of the money supply. The FOMC then instructs the Federal Reserve's big regional bank in New York to enforce its wishes through the New York banks' Open Market Account. Its officials are empowered to buy or sell for the Federal Reserve System government securities in dealings with private concerns that maintain markets in such issues.

If the FOMC has directed the manager of the Open Market Account in New York to pursue somewhat faster monetary growth, for example, he will normally order increased buying of securities by the Open Market Account. This buying tends to pump money from the Federal Reserve System into the private economy, as the New York Fed pays private sellers for the securities it buys. Conversely, when a tighter monetary policy is desired, the Open Market Account normally sells government securities. This serves to pull money out of the private economy into Federal Reserve coffers.

In brief, when the Federal Reserve buys securities in the open market, it creates bank reserves which did not exist before. The Fed makes payment simply by crediting the amount of its purchase to the account of the particular private bank involved in the transaction. Thus, money is created.

We have seen the key role that money plays in determining how much or how little inflation exists. And we have seen the key role that Washington plays—through the Fed's New York-based outlet—in actually creating money. It all appears very simple. If the Fed would merely tailor its moneymaking to a rate of increase compatible with inflation-free economic growth, a major inflationary force would quickly be reduced or even eliminated.

Unfortunately, the situation is not that simple.

* * *

For an idea of the complexity surrounding the matter of monetary growth, one should begin, perhaps, with the number four. Give or take a fraction of a percentage point, the number four—precisely, four percent—is the annual rate at which the U.S. economy has seemed able to expand over the long run. It is the average rate at which economic activity in the U.S.—gauged in terms of gross national product adjusted for price changes—actually has increased over many, many decades. And it is roughly the rate at which many authoritative analysts—surveying such basic considerations as the country's resources of labor and materials—estimate that the economy should be capable of expanding in coming decades.

Clearly, it is a basic economic consideration, to be weighed with care in policymaking deliberations in Washington. When analysts say that the economy has the ability to expand in the long run at a rate of about four percent annually, they are saying, in effect, that the nation's supply of goods and services has the ability to expand at a long-term rate of four percent annually. From this, it follows that money—the means by which goods and services may be purchased—should also grow at a long-term rate of roughly four percent a year.

One need not have majored in economics to detect that if the money supply year after year after year expands more rapidly than the economy can grow, prices will be driven upward. It is a simple matter, as noted earlier, of supply and demand. The supply of money expands in relation to the supply of goods and services. Conversely, if monetary growth repeatedly trails the ability of the economy to grow, prices will tend to decline. The supply of goods and services rises in relation to the availability of money.

Only twice in a recent 10-year stretch was money-supply growth less than the four percent deemed compatible with the economy's long-term capacity to expand. In the eight other years, monetary growth topped four percent. And in six of those years, it exceeded six percent. In 1972, an extreme illustration of the pattern, monetary expansion approximated nine percent, more than double the economy's potential growth rate. So accustomed have we become to monetary expansion rates in excess of four percent annually that when the money supply rose 4.7 percent in 1974, Federal Reserve authorities were characterized by many observers as pursuing a "tight" monetary policy.

As painful as it has been for many individuals, the worsening inflation of the past 10 years or so might be acceptable if it could be demonstrated clearly that the result has been a more swiftly growing economy, with reduced unemployment. Alas, there is no evidence to show that rapid monetary growth has produced anything but swifter inflation and the various economic distortions and dislocations that tend to emerge along with inflation. Indeed, it is a sad fact that the past decade has witnessed more economic trouble, including severe recessionary periods, than the preceding 10 years.

Perennially, the assumption Washington's economic planners has been that there will be time enough later to gear monetary expansion down to a pace that the economy, given its resources of labor and materials, can easily handle. But the question arises: When is "later"—next year, or the year after that, or the year after that?

Perhaps, ever so gradually, the average rate of monetary expansion can be brought down to a level at least remotely in line with the four percent figure. That appears to be the best hope, if inflation is finally to be subdued. But any such endeavor by policymakers will require a good deal more patience and perseverance than the history of the last 10 years suggests exists in Washington—no matter what political party happens to be in the driver's seat.

* * *

Several considerations further dim the prospects of any early return to noninflationary rates of monetary growth. One is the fundamental question of whether the economy's ability to grow in the long term may diminish in the years just ahead. Unfortunately, some business forecasters are convinced that over the next decade or so the economy's annual growth potential may well shrink below the four percent mark.

A U.S. Labor Department study, for example, forecasts a "sharp slowdown" in economic growth around the turn of the present decade, largely on account of demographic factors that should restrict labor-force growth. The study estimates that the economy's growth potential will drop around that time to about three percent annually from about four percent previously. Other analyses also stress the possible impact on growth of intensifying material-resource shortages. Oil, for example, is among many industrial building blocks, once taken for granted, that now increasingly must be used with care.

It follows, of course, that as the economy's ability to expand diminishes, so does the appropriate rate of monetary growth. By the time policymakers throttle back money-supply expansion to a four percent annual rate—if they ever manage to do so—they may find that three percent has become the appropriate level.

Of course, if overall economic activity happens to be enjoying an up-phase of the long-term business cycle, it becomes extra difficult for Federal Reserve officials to throttle monetary expansion. One reason is that as business activity increases, demand for bank loans tends to climb apace. And, as that transpires, the money supply tends to rise extra rapidly, whatever the intentions of the FOMC, through the multiplier effect described earlier in this chapter.

In addition, if economic activity accelerates, interest rates will likely tend to rise. This is the normal pattern when the economy has been in an up-phase of the business cycle for an appreciable length of time. However, any sharp increase in interest rates could hobble further economic growth and, in the process, exacerbate joblessness, a politically charged issue. Accordingly, much as they might wish to throttle back monetary expansion in such circumstances, Fed officials might not dare to do so, in the fear that any such effort would also force up interest rates so sharply as to crimp general economic growth.

A Congressional resolution cautions Fed officials against any restrictive moves on the monetary front that might also act to force interest rates higher. While the resolution aims specifically at monetary policy "in the first half of 1975," it seems bound to influence Federal Reserve attitudes continually. The resolution also talks vaguely about the importance of gearing monetary policy to "the economy's long-term potential to increase production." But nowhere in the resolution is there a mention of what that potential may be. The emphasis seems unmistakably on the virtue of keeping interest rates down in the short term.

Such considerations provide scant comfort for anyone hoping that the country's inflation problem may readily be whipped. That happy eventuality cannot arrive, experience makes plain, until policymakers begin to pay at least a modicum of attention to the importance of gearing monetary expansion to the economy's capacity to grow.

Quite apart from political considerations, there are serious technical questions about the Federal Reserve's ability to gear money-supply expansion to four percent annually or, for that matter, to any exact rate. There is, as noted, the underlying question of exactly what an appropriate rate of growth may be. Milton Friedman, whose writings include an exhaustive study of U.S. monetary trends, suggests that the optimum monetary growth rate in the U.S. very recently may have narrowed from four percent to as little as two percent yearly. The demographic factors cited by the Labor Department analysts, discussed earlier, partly explain Mr. Friedman's view. Other considerations range from the spread of service-type enterprises within the U.S. economy to the productivity-limiting impact of increasing efforts to curb industrial pollution.

Even if a sound judgment could be made that, say, four percent is the correct rate for U.S. monetary growth, a technical question arises over whether M-1—checking-account deposits plus currency in circulation—in fact constitutes the best monetary measure for Federal Reserve policymakers to follow. Actually, more than half a dozen gauges of the country's money supply have been devised by Washington statisticians. There is also, for example, M-2, which embraces all of M-1 plus savings-account deposits at commercial banks. And there is M-3, which embraces all of M-1 and M-2 and, in addition, savings-account deposits of various other thrift institutions besides commercial banks. Other, still more comprehensive gauges of the country's money supply take into account, for instance, holdings of various Treasury securities.

Which of the many M's should the FOMC be watching? No one can say for sure. In the past, the tendency has been to cencentrate on M-1. But recently M-2 and even M-3 have come under greater scrutiny. Perhaps this is a wise decision on the part of the FOMC. Perhaps it is M-3 that should be made to grow at, say, four percent annually. But for now that can only be speculation. Experience shows, it should be noted, that M-2 and M-3 tend to grow more rapidly than M-1. Thus, when M-1 expands at, say, only two percent a year, M-2 may well be rising at, say, four percent yearly. Altogether, it is a tricky, technical business, one that imposes new uncertainties atop the basic uncertainty of gearing monetary growth to the economy's potential.

An additional caveat: No statistic generated by Washington's number mills seems more subject to revision and revision and revision than the money supply. It is entirely possible, for example, that the FOMC may admirably succeed in gearing, say, M-1 to a desired annual growth of four percent—only to discover, after a belated revision of the numbers, that M-1's growth was really, say, six percent annually during the period in question.

* * *

On top of such problems, there is the difficulty posed by the question of monetary velocity. It is widely recognized that the money supply—whichever of the many M's is used—is a key factor in the inflation picture. However, the rate at which the money supply turns over can have an equally important influence on the price outlook. A one percent rise in the turnover of the money supply—monetary velocity—has the same effect on the overall economy as a one percent increase in the money supply. Monetary velocity can be precisely calculated by dividing the gross national product by the money supply at any particular time. The sum of money-supply expansion and velocity growth adds up to the rate of growth in the gross national product.

A study of monetary velocity has been conducted by William E. Gibson, an economist at Smith Barney, Harris Upham & Co., a New York-based securities concern. The bulk of increases in velocity, the study finds, are triggered by three factors.

One is a rise in interest rates. When interest rates increase, the expense of holding assets in the form of noninterest-bearing money rises. It pays to economize on money when interest rates increase, and so velocity tends to increase.

A second factor is a booming economy. Velocity grows more rapidly when the economy is in the expansion phase of the business cycle and it expands more slowly or actually falls during a recession. During economic up-phases, consumers generally feel much more carefree and, accordingly, attempt to get along with smaller balances of money in the bank per dollar of spending.

A third factor involves financial innovation. The introduction of such items as credit cards and overdraft facilities at thrift institutions induce people to finance many of their outlays using smaller bank-deposit balances. The result, again, is a tendency to increase monetary velocity and, ultimately, inflationary pressures within the economy.

Mr. Gibson goes on to warn that monetary velocity, despite such characteristics, is a gossamer concept, difficult for Washington's policymakers to pinpoint and allow for. With regard to velocity, the economist says, "everyone is flying blind." In sum, as if the Fed's task of wisely tailoring monetary growth to the economy's potential were not already tricky enough, there is the amorphous, but highly important, matter of velocity to be dealt with. Velocity, Mr. Gibson concludes, constitutes "a critical variable" in any fight to control inflation, but it is also, unfortunately, an extremely slippery, hard-to-manage variable.

* * *

Any discussion of the money supply and its role as an inflationary force within the economy would be incomplete without attention to the matter of debt monetization. What does that imposing phrase mean?

An explanation begins with the problem posed by federal budget deficits. Such deficits develop, naturally, when the federal government spends more than it takes in. When a deficit occurs, the U.S. Treasury Department is normally compelled to borrow funds in order to make up the government's financial shortage. This federal borrowing can occur in various ways. The Treasury can compete for money in the so-called open market, seeking to divert investors' funds that might otherwise be lent, say, to a private corporation also in need of funds. Such a competition for investment money obviously tends to drive up interest rates.

However, under law the Federal Reserve also can purchase government securities. The money managers at the Fed may fear the Treasury's borrowing needs are of such magnitude that interest rates in the open market may climb steeply, too steeply for the general health of business. Federal Reserve authorities, in such circumstances, could decide to purchase some or all of the securities that the Treasury is trying to sell to raise money to meet the Federal budget deficit.

Now to the phrase "monetizing the debt," which is the

phrase that economists apply to this process. And it is indeed an appropriate description. The upshot of such action by the Fed is to create new money within the economy. The procedure may relieve interest-rate pressures for the time being. But in the longer run, inflationary forces are generated —precisely because, as we have seen, money-supply increases ultimately act to push up prices. Interest rates tend to rise as well, as lenders struggle, with higher and higher prices, to protect the long-term value of their loans.

The pressures that large federal deficits can exert on FOMC decisions are enormous. Albert T. Sommers, chief economist of the Conference Board, feels that this pressure is so large that it virtually eliminates the freedom of action of monetary policymakers. He puts the situation thus: "The ultimate causes of inflation are upstream from monetary policy. Money is not the prime mover of inflation but a link in a causal chain. No conceivable behavior of the monetary authorities can hope to reach up the chain and reverse the processes" in which inflation is born.

Paramount among these "processes," the Conference Board official makes clear, are the country's perennial budget deficits. He estimates that in the years 1975 to 1979 the accumulated federal budget deficit should amount to "a spectacular $285 billion give or take a dozen billion." Political pressures that lead to such massive red ink are detailed and assessed elsewhere in this book. Whatever they may be, however justified the red ink, the painful fact is that the already difficult job of gearing monetary growth to the economy's natural ability to expand is further complicated.

CHAPTER NINE

A Trap to Avoid

The dimensions of the economic dilemma now facing Americans are great indeed. There is the painful bite of inflation. There is the distressing waste caused by unemployment. And there is the devilish business of attempting somehow to correct one without aggravating the other. It is entirely understandable that the men and women who determine economic policy in Washington should make every effort to resolve the situation. At the same time, however, it is most important that clear hazards be recognized, that dangerous traps be avoided. Seemingly sensible solutions may turn out, on close inspection, not to be so.

The idea, at first glance, appears reasonable enough. The economy suffers from inflation and unemployment. To cure the unemployment, clearly, a move to stimulate economic policy must be pursued. Governmental spending must be increased sharply. A more rapid expansion of the nation's money supply must be initiated. This will quicken the economic pace, and, in the process, jobs will proliferate still more rapidly, unemployment will inevitably dwindle.

But what about the dilemma's other horn? Won't inflation

surely worsen in such an economic climate? Of course it will—without some action aimed directly at preventing such a spiral.

What sort of action?

In a complicated era that welcomes simple, direct solutions to sticky problems, there is an understandable tendency to adopt a sanguine view of governmental controls—over prices, over wages, over other aspects of economic activity bearing upon the matter of inflation and joblessness. Clamp on controls and then proceed to spur the economy along, trimming joblessness, yet preventing the inflation that surely would otherwise erupt.

It is a wonderfully appealing idea in a time such as this. It is so enticing, in fact, that it demands close scrutiny. The idea of resorting to controls to solve America's great dilemma contains so much surface appeal, in fact, that a concise effort should be made to expose how very bad the notion really is.

* * *

The idea of somehow curing the country's economic illnesses through the implementation of various control measures remains remarkably beguiling, notwithstanding the sorry history of such programs. As recently as mid-1974, a Gallup poll showed that most Americans favored the reimposition of wage-price controls—even though the controls program launched three years earlier by President Nixon was a shambles. "The public feels there should be more, not less control," observed C. Jackson Grayson, head of Mr. Nixon's Price Commission, after the three-year program ended. Hendrik Houthakker, a Harvard economist, similarly has remarked: "Most people believe in controls, and in a democracy this is a factor which no one would want to ignore.

To some extent the government has given the people what they want" in the Nixon controls program.

Why? Why, in a country where individual freedom is revered, do so many citizens hold so kindly a view of controls?

Milton Friedman has warned: "If the U.S. ever succumbs to collectivism, to government control over every facet of our lives, it will not be because the Socialists win any arguments. It will be through the indirect route of wage and price controls."

The success of America's remarkable effort to conduct governmental affairs in a democratic fashion, in the long run, must depend on the perspicacity of the population. In some areas this ingredient is plainly apparent—as, for example, in the public's admirable refusal to be misled over the years by political adventurers, such as Wisconsin's Senator Joseph McCarthy.

In other areas, however, a dangerous naiveté is apparent, and nowhere is this more evident than in the field of wage-price control. Inflation is painful. Unemployment is painful. How simple it would be to set things right by merely having the government forbid price increases and wage boosts. After all, wages and prices were placed under control during World War II and the Korean War, with a limited degree of success. After all, such noted authors as John Kenneth Galbraith, the Harvard economist, have long argued the merits of wage-price control.

* * *

President Carter stated his position with regard to wage-price controls during a press conference held on December

3, 1976, just after he had defeated Gerry Ford for the White House.

A reporter asked: "During the campaign you said you didn't want to use wage and price controls but that standby authority might be something that you would consider. I believe earlier today you said flatly that you would not request standby wage and price control authority during your administration. What made you change your mind?"

President Carter answered: "I have no intention of asking the Congress to give me standby wage and price controls and have no intention of imposing wage and price controls in the next four years. If some national emergency should arise, and I think that's a very remote possibility, that would be the only indication I can see for a need for wage and price controls. I believe that the primary threat in these next four years is continued unemployment, and I believe with strong leadership, with my appealing to both industry and business on one hand and labor on the other to show constraint, that an adequate mutual responsibility will be assumed and unnecessary increases of prices and wages can be avoided. So I don't see any possibility or advisability of my asking for wage and price control authority."

The reporter persisted: "In light of the fact that the consumer-price index went up six-tenths of a point today—it's the third time in three months that it's risen dramatically—I still don't understand what the purpose of not having standby authority might be. You need not use it unless you want to."

Mr. Carter curtly responded:: "Well, I can't continue with you about it. My statement stands. I don't believe that I will need standby wage and price authority. I believe in a free-market system and always have. And I believe that the constant threat of wage and price controls is sometimes a stimulation for unwarranted increases in wages and prices, and I want to remove that threat completely from business and labor and form a partnership with them so that we mutually can be responsible for the avoiding of unwarranted increases. That's one of the factors that might perhaps help to answer your question."

* * *

It is easy to see what Mr. Carter had in mind by saying that threat of controls "is sometimes a stimulation for unwarranted increases in wages and prices." Shortly after that particular press conference, Irwin Kellner, a vice president for economics at New York's Manufacturers Hanover Trust, dispensed some noteworthy advice for his business clients. Mr. Kellner expressed a concern that the Carter administration, notwithstanding the press-conference position, would ultimately impose wage-price controls. Accordingly, the economist urged businessmen to "raise list prices now." He went on: "It's naive to think that, somehow, failure to raise posted prices is unpatriotic. There are a handful of businesses that do hold such a position, but they're ignoring their responsibility to employees and shareholders."

How many executives acted on that advice is not known. But the statement offers a clear example of how the very threat of controls can induce inflation that might otherwise not occur. The same tendency, of course, applies to wage demands. If they believe that wages will be frozen in a year's time, union negotiators understandably will press for especially large pay boosts in a contract coming up for renewal.

We see, then, that the mere threat of a controls program can aggravate inflation, as businesses move to raise their prices and unions their wage rates before a wage-price lid is clamped down.

But the trouble with controls extends far beyond this anticipatory problem. A 1977 study by economists at Morgan Guaranty Trust in New York probed some other hazardous aspects. "The most obvious cost of a controls program is inefficiency produced by the added distortions to the price system," the study warns.

> The importance of prices in allocating capital investment and in determining how much of millions of different goods and services is produced needs no repetition. What is often underestimated is what is lost when a non-market method of price determination is substituted for a market system. A vast amount of information is applied to economic decisions when a market system is used to determine prices. Information about consumer preferences, the costs of various production techniques, and a multitude of judgments about future changes in technology and preferences are only a few of the factors which are simultaneously and continuously being appraised and acted on through the price system to shape investment, production and consumption decisions.

While the Morgan Guaranty study is mainly limited to the matter of price controls, much of the commentary may be applied equally to wage controls. Just as "the price system" of the marketplace is distorted, with consequent "inefficiency," so of course is the system by which most wages are ultimately determined. As in the case of prices, controls on wages create "an additional problem . . . of equity," the report concludes. "Workers whose incomes are adversely affected by controls will inevitably feel that they have been unjustly singled out."

Beryl W. Sprinkel, executive vice president and chief economist of Harris Trust and Savings Bank in Chicago, says bluntly that "price and wage controls do not work." They just might occasionally work, we submit, if a country is willing to turn itself into a police state, with harsh penalties for wage-price violators, or if a country is enmeshed in a major war effort, one widely supported by the citizenry. But neither situation—happily—applies currently in the U.S.

* * *

This is perhaps an appropriate moment to take note of the argument, occasionally voiced, that the dilemma of inflation and unemployment seems not to trouble centrally-planned Communist economies. The argument is specious. Inflation and unemployment assume different guises in different societies. In America, as in most of Western Europe and large portions of the Far East, inflation is manifest in the various indexes used to monitor price trends. Unemployment is apparent in other indexes that pinpoint jobless members of the population.

Not so in the centrally planned societies. In the Soviet Union, as well as the satellite Communist nations of Europe, inflation can generally be seen not through any price index, but in a frustrating unavailability of goods and services. Better that an item be available at a price that is possibly inflated than not be available at all. A few statistics help illustrate the form that inflation has taken, for example, in the Soviet Union. In the U.S., there is about one automobile for every two persons, while only one in 64 Russians owns a car.

For each Soviet household that owns a refrigerator, eight U.S. families own one. There is one TV set for every two Americans, but only one TV per five Russian citizens. In the housing industry, a vivid contrast is evident. An American on the average, boasts about 150 percent more living space than a Russian. And the typical American family owns a house with some land. The typical Russian family resides in a cramped, crowded apartment.

Russian price levels are set by the Soviet government, of course, rather than through marketplace forces. The shortages that persist in Russia—and the situation is similiar elsewhere in the Communist world—are clearly a form of inflation. The price may be right, but the product simply isn't available. A major expansion in Soviet production schedules would obviously serve to ease such scarcity. However, a glance at some Soviet output statistics shows no such surge. In a recent 12-month period, Russia produced 1.2 million cars, or roughly 10 percent of the comparable U.S. auto production. A footnote: the 1.2 million cars produced in Russia approximates American auto production all the way back in 1916. The picture is much the same in other areas. In the same 12 months, Russian output of washing machines, at about three million units, was barely over half of the corresponding U.S. total.

A few additional figures are worthy of note. The average American car buyer must work about seven months to earn the wherewithal to buy a small automobile. The average Russian car buyer must work about 38 months—more than five times as long—for his small car.

In one area, however, Russian consumers are ahead of their American counterparts. The average Russian consumes nearly nine quarts of liquor a year. That's twice as much as the Americans, the world's next biggest drinkers, on the average, consume.

Like inflation, unemployment assumes a somewhat different guise in Communist lands. In theory, there is no problem. But in fact, the problem is large indeed. There is without question a distressing amount of underemployment throughout the Socialist world. This widespread underemployment—using three workers to perform tasks handled by one in, say, the U.S.—tends to hold jobless levels below where they might otherwise be. But in the process living standards also are kept down. Moreover, studies suggest that, even with the underemployment, considerable—though unreported—joblessness exists in Russia and its Communist neighbors. Roughly 30 percent of the Soviet work force is engaged in farming, compared with about 5 percent in the U.S. It would be a simple matter to reduce unemployment in American cities by sending all jobless urban dwellers out to farms in the Midwest and elsewhere, armed with a rake and a hoe. But that would hardly constitute a practical, lasting solution to America's unemployment problem. And, of course, it could add a huge amount of steam to the country's already painful price spiral.

Altogether, the record in Socialist countries makes plain that tight governmental regulation of the economic marketplace—of price and wage negotiations—in no way solves problems of inflation and joblessness. Rather, the symptoms of the illness are merely altered in especially painful ways.

* * *

The continuing public admiration for wage-price controls persists, it should be added, in the face of an unrelievedly dismal history. They did not succeed as long ago as 1800 B.C., the history books show. This was the time of Hammurabi, the ruler of ancient Babylonia. His controls program was part of a diverse legal code that survived, not entirely successfully, for some 1500 years. The penalties prescribed included death—by drowning, as it happened—for any merchant so foolish as to raise his prices or his wage payments more rapidly than the controls program allowed. The main lesson for today in Hammurabi's experiment is that wage-price controls ultimately fail, even when the harshest of penalties are applied. In a 1964 book titled *Babylon* by James MacQueen, we find, for instance, the unfortunate example of a tavernkeeper who ignored a control order pricing six measures of liquor at five measures of corn. The tavernkeeper attempted instead to collect silver, worth considerably more than the corn, for his liquor. When authorities finally discovered this, the sentence was swift—death by drowning.

Georges Contenau, in his 1954 book titled *Everyday Life in Babylon and Assyria,* paints a dismal picture of ancient efforts to fix wages and prices. For example, he writes that the ancient lawmakers "made several attempts to fix prices, but a closer examination makes it clear that any success they may have had was quite fortuitous and that they were doing no more than recording with satisfaction the low prices of certain commodities, while the rest of their calculations were no more than good intentions more or less divorced from reality." One of the few successes of Hammurabi's controls program involved Babylonian oxen. The price of a good Babylonian ox remained at approximately 20 shekels for several centuries.

Mark Skousen, in a recent book called *Playing the Price Controls Game,* devotes considerable attention to the sorry history of wage-price efforts through the ages. His finding is that such efforts have never been made to work successfully for an appreciable time. The record is particularly dismal during periods of peace and in relatively free societies. He recalls, for example, that after the code of Hammurabi, the Athenians clamped "severe controls on the grain trade" in the fourth century B.C. Inspectors were engaged to enforce the program. As in Babylonia, death was the punishment for violators.

During the time of the Roman Empire, a strenuous effort to impose a successful controls program was launched by the Emperor Diocletian. He tried to fix the prices of some 800 different items and also proclaimed wage ceilings in his so-called edict of A.D. 301. Among those affected were tailors, doctors, bricklayers, writers, teachers and lawyers. The ancient program foreshadowed increasingly complex controls programs of the recent past. It embraced more than 220 price schedules for food items, 87 for hides and leather goods, 94 for timber and wood products, 385 for textiles, 32 for various grass products, 53 for cosmetics, ointments and incense and 17 for precious metals. This elaborate effort limped along for 13 years before it was finally given up.

An ancient historian, Lactantius, had this to say about the demise of the Emperor's program:

> After that, the many oppressions which he put in practice had brought a general dearth upon the empire. Then he set himself to regulate the prices of all vendable things. There was also much bloodshed upon very slight and trifling accounts, and people brought provisions no more to markets, since they could not get a reasonable price for them. This increased the dearth so much that at last after many had died by it, the law itself was set aside.

Such laws continue to be implemented again and again. Only 60 years after the demise of the Diocletian wage-price program, the Roman Emperor Julian launched a similar endeavor. Again, after a brief interval, the unmanageable program had to be abandoned.

Controls programs kept popping up in various areas during the Middle Ages. The British attempted to control the retail and wholesale price of wine as long ago as 1199. The effort failed. An unsuccessful effort to control the price of British wheat and bread was made three years later. In Holland, when Antwerp was besieged by the Duke of Parma during the 1580's, a wide-ranging price-control program was established. It failed dismally. Indeed, historians recall that the program served only to aggravate commodity shortages initially caused by siege of the city. Other long-ago programs existed in such diverse areas as India, France and Mongolia. Kubla Khan assigned price ceilings to a wide variety of products.

* * *

A country mentioned earlier in this book for its horrendous inflation during the early 1920's, Germany, also over the years has dabbled a great deal in price-control programs. Adolph Hitler was an early advocate of wage-price regulations. Indeed, Mark Skousen maintains that "many of the modern techniques used to enforce controls were developed by the Nazi dictator." In November 1936, he implemented a "price-stop" decree whose regulations amounted to a rollback of most prices to month-earlier levels. Later, the Nazis initiated control techniques aimed at preventing the substitution of inferior merchandise at old price levels. Also, the Nazis launched the now-familiar idea of allowing "pass-throughs" of cost increases. Penalties for violation of the rules included the confiscation of a person's property and, in some instances, death. Even so, the Nazi program was hardly a resounding success. Of course, as World War II developed, severe shortages of all sorts plagued the Third Reich. The controls program, along with the German economy in general, was soon a shambles.

After the war, the Allied authorities implemented a wage-price freeze in the beaten country. This only worsened the German economic plight. Barter became a way of life on both sides of the now-divided nation. The role of cigarettes took on a new significance, as an article in the British newspaper *Sunday Express* explains. Germany, it states, was a land

> almost run on cigarettes. Seventy-five percent of everyday crime in the country is traceable to cigarettes. . . . You can't throw a cigarette stump away without someone diving into the road to pick it up. Nearly everybody does it, no matter of what social position. . . . A large percentage of the German cigarette buyers are women. At times, they become quite maniacal, selling their children's food, their belongings and even themselves to get cigarettes. One cannot possibly imagine the lengths to which people who lack tobacco will go to get a smoke. It is far worse than hunger.

The remarkable postwar economic resurgence of West Germany, which began under the guidance of Ludwig Erhard, can be traced to the country's abandonment, with reluctant Allied approval, of its cumbersome controls regulations. Had the controls not been lifted, it seems most probable in retrospect that the country's postwar "economic miracle" would not have occurred.

While it may be more disastrous than most, the German encounter with wage-price controls is by no means unique in Europe. There is, for example, the post-World War II experience of the United Kingdom. In 1948, the country's new Labour government decided to freeze wages, as well as corporate dividend payments. But the program was farcical. Enforcement was nonexistent. A major reason: the country was at last at peace. As a result the effort was abandoned by 1950, amid spiraling wage and price levels.

Since then other British governments have made all sorts of further efforts—also unsuccessful—to clamp various lids on prices and wages. A National Incomes Commission was inaugurated in 1962, but was ineffective. In 1964 a National Board for Prices and Income came along. Again, the effect was minimal, as wages and prices continued to climb. In 1966, the British government introduced a six-month freeze of wages, prices and dividends. The effort was unsuccessful. In 1972 the Conservative party, by then in power, imposed a 90-day wage-price freeze and then extended the freeze. Again, the effort failed. Indeed, it served merely as a prelude to a horrendous period of inflation within Britain. In some months, the country's consumer-price index climbed at rates exceeding 20 percent annually. Such a pace would cut the value of the British pound in half within only three-and-a-half years.

France and Italy, Britain's fellow Common Market members, also have resorted again and again to wage-price controls during the postwar years. Again and again, the programs have failed. Sometimes a bit of comedy has surfaced.

In the fall of 1977, a "croissant war" developed in Paris, the direct result of a French government move to try to freeze some food prices. Butchers, bakers, fishmongers and restaurateurs, protesting the freeze, closed their facilities. Among foods whose prices were supposedly frozen were the crescent-shaped rolls that Frenchmen consume with their coffee at breakfast. According to the freeze plan, the croissants were to be sold for no more than one franc or about 20 cents. The "war" between the angry, striking bakers and the government price regulators was eventually won—predictably—by the irate bakers. For the French, the prospect of doing without their morning croissants far outweighed any government price-fixing ideas.

In Holland strict price controls were imposed in the early 1950's. Late in the decade restraints were extended to cover wage increases as well. The effort failed and, in 1968, the control apparatus was scrapped. Norway and Sweden each attempted to freeze prices in 1971. The programs appeared to work for a few months but then collapsed. A wage-price explosion ensued in each country after the price-lid flew off. Finland and Denmark are among other European countries that have flirted—unsuccessfully—with wage-price constraints in recent years.

Asia, it should be added, also shows a sorry history of wage-price programs. Some historians blame the downfall of Chiang Kai-shek in part on his determination to impose strict wage and price controls at a time when his beleaguered government was amassing huge budget deficits and pursuing a highly inflationary monetary policy. The inevitable result of this ill-timed control effort was a severe shortage of most items. Chiang attempted to hold the line by intensifying penalties for violators—for example, by executing black marketeers publicly. The harsh measures were to no avail. Violations continued, and, understandably, Chiang swiftly lost the backing of many merchants and other businessmen. Soon thereafter the Chinese Communists gained control over the sprawling nation, which they still rule.

* * *

The North American continent has experienced its share of misadventures with various controls efforts. In 1975, Canada's Prime Minister Pierre Trudeau pushed through an "incomes policy" that eventually required 6,000 companies to file reports with an Anti-Inflation Board. The reports not only involved price levels but profits, dividends and wage payments. Corporations found to have excessive cash reserves were ordered to cut their prices and absorb most of their costs.

At the start of the plan, Canada's overall price level was rising at about 11 percent a year. Mr. Trudeau hoped that under the program this rise would be trimmed to only four percent annually within three years. But no sooner was the program under way than problems began to arise. Jean-Luc Pepin, chairman of the Anti-Inflation Board, confidently announced: "It is expected that Canadians will voluntarily abide by the guidelines and cooperate with the board so that the need to use the enforcement powers will not frequently arise." The board's staff at this point numbered no more than 60 persons, so that voluntary cooperation was clearly essential. However, at the very start the regulations began to crumble. Some 22,000 Canadian postal clerks demanded and received, with impunity, a 38 percent pay increase from the government—despite a rule calling for an approximate 10 percent a year ceiling on pay boosts. At the same time, after angry protests and a realization of the enforcement difficulty involved, the government decided to exempt various food and farm products, hardly inconsequential items in any fight to reduce inflation.

Within two years after its implementation, more than a year before its scheduled expiration, the Canadian program was tottering. At the start of 1978, the country's rate of inflation was still close to nine percent annually. In fact, Canada's program to curb inflation during the two years of controls was considerably less successful than concurrent efforts in the U.S., where no such controls programs was in effect at the time.

While Canadian inflation was little eased by controls, other aspects of the country's economic situation were adversely affected.

A correspondent for *Business Week,* writing from Ottawa, bluntly concluded that Canada's "economic problems stem from the controls program instituted to stabilize the economy." The Canadian unemployment rate at the start of 1978 was approximately as high as the rate of inflation, roughly nine percent of the labor force. Overall economic growth for the year amounted to only about two percent, less than half the previous year's rate and less than half the comparable growth rate in the neighboring U.S. Direct foreign investment in Canada had been averaging an inflow of $1 billion annually when the controls program was initiated. After the program, a yearly investment outflow of $1 billion developed. "Investors not only don't want in here," observed a prominent Canadian economist in late 1977. "Those in want out." Along the same line, Lawrence J. Murphy, a Canadian specialist at the Conference Board, recalls that business-capital investment within Canada "came to a screeching halt" on account of investors' antipathy toward the program. It is noteworthy that in October 1977 the value of the Canadian dollar in terms of its none-too-robust U.S. counterpart hit a 40-year low.

By the end of 1977, the staff of Canada's Anti-Inflation Board had mushroomed from the original 60 persons to nearly 10 times that number. Yet, the backlog of cases involving possible violations and requiring a board ruling was in the thousands. Rulings often were not handed down until many months after wage agreements were negotiated. Nearly 4,000 such cases were listed as "in progress."

At the same time, many interruptions in production occurred. For instance, output at a group of Montreal flour mills was disrupted for the better part of a year because workers there objected to a ruling that lowered a negotiated wage increase.

Not surprisingly, in the closing weeks of 1977, long before the scheduled expiration of the program, the Canadian government promised to dismantle its unhappy experimental controls. In addition, it announced a plan to cut taxes and increase investment incentives in a belated effort to get the country's economy rolling again.

* * *

Hardly happier than the Canadian experience is experience with controls in the U.S. Such efforts, in fact, have been launched periodically throughout U.S. history. Early American colonists resorted to price ceilings on various agricultural products from time to time. The efforts invariably failed, even though Americans who violated the rules were denounced as "adulterers and whoremongers," according to one colonial history. Norman Skousen recalls in his book that "many state and local governments continued to enforce price controls during the Revolutionary War." Boston, for example, published the names of violators as "enemies" of the country and according to an order by local authorities, urged that the public "abstain from all trade and conversation with them, and the people at large inflict upon them that punishment which such wretches deserve." Nonetheless, Mr. Skousen reports, "fines, threats and boycotts did not stem the tide of rising prices and the flood of paper money during this period."

In 1780, with evidence aplenty that such efforts did not seem to work, the new U.S. Congress produced this resolution: "It hath been found by experience that limitations upon the prices of commodities are not only ineffectual for the purposes proposed, but likewise productive of very evil consequences to the great detriment of the public service and grievous oppression of individuals."

A major controls effort was instituted in the U.S. during World War I. A Price-Fixing Committee, for example, was established to try to set prices of commodities viewed as basic to the war effort. Because a spirit of wartime sacrifice prevailed, the program met with some limited success. Similarly, in World War II, a pervasive program to control wage-price levels was moderately successful on account of widespread public support of any government measures aimed at bolstering the general war effort. Even so, the program at one point necessitated 68,000 full-time employees at various governmental agencies, plus another 40,000 part-time price-watchers, as they were known. And even this vast civilian army of controllers proved insufficient to prevent active black markets in such key items as tires, meat, gasoline and sugar.

In a book titled *The Black Market*, Marshall Clinard, wrote:

> By June of 1944 there had been over 640 robberies of local boards involving 300,000,000 gallons [of gasoline] in coupons, and about the same time a campaign against counterfeit coupons enabled the identification of 132 different types of gasoline counterfeits and yielded 13 printing presses used to print counterfeits. One such press was running an order for 15 million counterfeit "A" gas coupons and for 1.5 million counterfeit shoe coupons when found. In one case, a racketeer with a prison record for robbery was found illegally in possession of 38,000 gallons in counterfeit gasoline coupons, 25,000 gallons in genuine fuel oil coupons, and 437 counterfeit shoe coupons, as well as a loaded automatic, two shotguns, and burglary tools.

Not surprisingly, the controls program collapsed soon after the Japanese surrender in August 1945.

Again, patriotism accounted for whatever limited success was achieved by a governmental effort to control wages and prices during the Korean War. And again the effort was marred by the emergence of widespread black-marketeering.

Perhaps the most pathetic U.S. attempt to control wage and price increases was that launched by President Nixon in 1971. First, Mr. Nixon and his associates imposed a 90-day freeze on wages, prices and rents. He appointed a Cost of Living Council to carry out the program. Fines up to $5,000 were established for violations. Then, under a so-called Phase II of the program—a 60-day affair—some limited increases were allowed. Then came a six-month Phase III plan during which constraints were further eased. There followed

Phase III-½, a second freeze attempt, this time for only 60 days. And finally, before the tottering effort collapsed entirely, a Phase IV was initiated from August 1973 through April 1974.

Some brief statistics sum up the ineffectiveness of all this regulating endeavor. In August 1971 the country's index of consumer prices stood at 122.1 (on a 1967 base of 100). In May 1974, after nearly three years of controls of one sort or another, the same price index stood at 145.5. During the same period, the average hourly compensation of all workers in private businesses in the U.S. soared from 130 (on a 1967 base of 100) to nearly 160. Moreover, by the end of Phase IV, widespread shortages of all varieties had developed. By one survey, 97 percent of U.S. corporations were experiencing "unusual difficulties" in obtaining essential supplies. The U.S. economy, meanwhile, was slipping deeper and deeper into its worst slump in many respects since the Depression years before World War II. When the economy finally began to turn up again in the spring of 1975 Mr. Nixon's effort to impose controls was only a sorry memory.

* * *

Notwithstanding the record of controls in the U.S. and abroad, there can be little doubt that the threat remains of still another government stab at fixing wage and price levels. As noted, the idea still commands wide public support. "A bout with wage-price controls is inevitable sometime in the next decade," says Paul Samuleson, the Nobel-laureate economist at the Massachusetts Institute of Technology. He elaborates: "They work in the short term—although admittedly, that short run has to be pretty short. We'll be seeing a stop-and-go economy over the next 10 years. Inflation, controls and recession are all in the cards. But I'm uncertain of timing."

Milton Friedman concurs: "It would be premature to suppose that we have truly learned our lesson. Price controls have been imposed repeatedly for more than 2,000 years. They have always failed, yet they have been repeatedly resurrected—I doubt that we in the United States have seen the last of price and wage controls."

Some influential economists still sing the praises of wage-price controls, despite the lamentable record. One is John Kenneth Galbraith, the prolific author and Harvard economist. He steadfastly asserts that price controls "have an important and perhaps indispensable place in the pharmacopoeia of inflation remedies." And he contends that a successful controls program would "need not apply to more than a few thousand of the largest firms."

This suggestion strikes Mr. Friedman, among others, as dangerously naive. The idea that controlling a relatively small number of strategic prices will suffice to control the price level in general, he warns, "seems impervious to the evidence that prices in products produced by the concentrated industries have on the average risen less rapidly than other products or indeed may have fallen." He adds: "It is equally impervious to the evidence that wages of unionized labor typically lag behind wages of nonunionized labor in the early stages of an accelerated inflation, and catch up only later."

A particularly damaging sort of price-control program, it should be noted, lingers on in the U.S.—in New York City. It is the city's rent-control program. The rent-control program was allowed to continue after other World War II price ceilings were lifted. The troubled city's leaders over the postwar decades lacked the political guts to scrap the program, even though many of the protected tenants—those who stay put—are New Yorkers bringing home yearly salaries that range well above $50,000. The late Richard Stone, a highly perceptive real-estate reporter for *The Wall Street Journal*, in the early 1970's had this to say of New York's rent-control program: "The dimensions of the New York [housing] shortage are vast. The rental vacancy rate is below one percent. Private construction is near paralysis. Increasing numbers of landlords simply give up, abandoning buildings they neither can afford to maintain nor can sell at any price. Tenants left with no heat, water, or electricity vacate such buildings in a matter of days. When that happens, blight swallows up whole neighborhoods almost overnight." The culprit, Mr. Stone concluded, was "New York's archaic rent-control law."

Along the same line, Paul Samuelson has written: "New York City rent controls do favor those lucky enough to find a cheap apartment, but they inhibit new private building in low-cost housing and they discourage economies of space utilization that high rents tend to induce."

Altogether, as New York City's stubborn adherence to rent controls may suggest, the possibility remains strong that the country generally may turn again to wage-price controls in an effort to resolve its continuing inflation-unemployment dilemma. It is a "solution" that simply will not work. It will in all likelihood only worsen the situation. It should be eschewed, however alluring it may seem at a glance, however much some political leaders or economists may commend the idea.

Norman Skousen warns that "when inflation flares again—and I am fairly confident that it will—the general public will be the most vocal group calling for new controls. Businessmen and labor leaders in general may be reluctant to give their support, but they will probably give in, hoping for some benefits in return." Whatever "benefits" they may reap most definitely will be more than offset by the misery that still another stab at controls would cause for the economy and the population in general.

CHAPTER TEN

Dealing with Government

Resolving the dilemma of the country's unwanted economic twins—unemployment and inflation—necessitates appreciating, as a first step, precisely what is involved. We have seen that the painfully high rate of unemployment, as distressing as it may be, constitutes a somewhat distorted reflection of America's actual labor scene. The much-publicized monthly jobless rate tends to paint an overly dismal picture of the real situation. An amazing proliferaiton of jobs has, by the same token, attracted lamentably scarce notice. We have also seen that the ravages of inflation in recent years have, if anything, been underestimated. We have glimpsed inflation's little-mentioned dark side. And we have inspected the many and diverse considerations that serve to keep the general price level moving swiftly, inexorably upward.

In brief, we have seen that the true nature of the country's unemployment-inflation bind is substantially different from the widely advertised, widely accepted image. A careful consideration of facts, we have seen, suggests that the inflation part of the dilemma requires even more attention than one might suppose necessary, and the unemployment side perhaps appreciably less attention than might be supposed.

However, gaining a proper perspective amounts merely to a beginning. Coping fully with the dilemma of unemployment and inflation requires an array of difficult decisions. Not the least of these, as this chapter will attempt to illustrate, involves the government itself. The previous chapter underlined the importance of eschewing the tempting but treacherous path of governmental wage-price controls. This chapter will proceed from there to examine broadly the existing ways in which governmental activity already serves to aggravate unemployment and inflation. In the process, corrective measures will be indicated.

A discussion of the expanding governmental role, particularly within the tax arena, appeared in Chapter Seven. The full dimensions of the government's economic presence, however, transcend taxes, vast governmental employment rolls and other familiar yardsticks of federal clout. A hard, close look at the governmental presence shows a pervasive economic involvement that, at once, acts to worsen both inflation and unemployment.

* * *

The governmental presence, its dimensions and its growth, can readily be documented. Within the legislative branch there are, of course, 100 senators and 435 members of the House of Representatives. But there are also 38,000 employees of congressmen and such legislative service agencies as the General Accounting Office, the Government Printing Office, the Congressional Budget Office and the Library of Congress. Within the Senate are 130 committees and subcommittees. Within the House are 211 committees and subcommittees. There are 14 so-called joint or special Congressional committees.

The executive branch, of course, is headed by the President. After him follow the Vice President, the White House staff, some 50 presidential advisory committees, 18 agencies, the various, massive cabinet departments, including 335 subagencies, 766 advisory committees, such executive agencies as the U.S. Postal Service and the Federal Reserve System, 54 additional independent executive agencies with 66 subagencies and 363 advisory committees and a host of other organizations—18 wholly owned federal corporations, 12 mixed ownership governmental corporations, 200-plus interagency and interdepartmental committees, nine quasi-official federal organizations, 58 additional committees, commissions and boards, and 91 international organizations to which the U.S. belongs.

Finally, there is the judicial branch of government. It encompasses the Supreme Court with its nine justices, more than 12,200 judges and judicial employees, 11 U.S. Courts of Appeal with 97 judges, 94 U.S. District Courts with 398 judges, the U.S. Court of Claims with 10 judges, the U.S. Tax Court with 19 judges, the U.S. Court of Customs and Patent Appeal with six judges and the U.S. Customs Court with one dozen judges.

In all, this vast federal structure of government embraces more than 2.8 million officeholders and employees. Nearly three million Americans, then, work at the federal level of government to help govern some 220 million Americans. This vast bureaucratic army of civilians is by no means restricted to the confines of Washington, D.C. Some 58,000 federal government employees toil, for example, in the State of Washington, some 298,000 in California, 25,300 in Hawaii, 172,300 in New York, 78,500 in Florida, 149,700 in Texas. The California figure, in fact, exceeds the Washington, D.C., total of 202,400. In addition to all these federal workers are more than two million members of the armed forces on duty throughout the U.S. and abroad.

This pervasive governmental presence, much as it has expanded in recent decades, threatens to keep growing in coming years. Curbing this growth—indeed, bringing about a reversal of this long-term trend—constitutes a most difficult challenge for the country. Yet, dealing with the unemployment-inflation bind demands precisely such an endeavor. If governmental growth can be curbed, if governmental involvement in all sorts of business matters can be cut back, a major step will have been taken in tackling the economy's dilemma.

This task will not be easy. It is no simple matter, for example, to convince skeptical citizens that a government continually promising to deal with inflation and unemployment must, in fact, be dealt with itself if the two economic problems are to be resolved. The momentum of an expanding governmental presence is considerable. It can be glimpsed in a variety of ways. Walter Wriston, highly articulate chairman of New York's Citicorp, has warned that "the road to serfdom is paved with demands for governments to take over more and more economic activity." Americans are decidedly not serfs, but they clearly are deeply troubled by the country's recent economic performance. Louis Brandeis, the late Supreme Court Justice, declared a half century ago that "experience should teach us to be most on our guard to protect liberty when government's purposes are beneficent; the greatest dangers to liberty lurk in insidious encroachment by men of zeal, well-meaning but without understanding." Justice Brandeis was concerned about the growth of government likely to develop as a result of New Deal programs of the early 1930's. What might he say today? At the time of his warning, the government accounted for some 10 percent of the nation's yearly output of goods and services. Today, the comparable percentage stands at roughly 40 percent.

* * *

Notwithstanding such an expansion, influential voices continue to urge a still larger governmental role in the economy. One such voice is that of Ralph Nader, the consumer advocate. A 1977 study by *Fortune* magazine found that some 60 of Nader's Raiders, as his followers are called, had "assumed control of many domestic-policy centers in the federal government." The list included Jimmy Carter's chief speechwriter, 13 other key White House assistants, four assistant attorneys general in the Justice Department, and assistant secretaries in each of the departments of Health, Education and Welfare, Commerce, Interior, Agriculture and Housing and Urban Development. Reasonably typical of such individuals is Jerry Jasinowski, an assistant secretary in the Commerce Department. Mr. Jasinowski makes clear that he staunchly supports greater, rather than less, governmental involvement on various economic fronts. He was, for example, an early advocate of a sharply higher, more inclusive hourly minimum wage. It is precisely such legislation, of course, that tends to aggravate national unemployment, particularly among the young and the black.

Significantly, before his appointment to his Commerce Department post, Mr. Jasinowski served as an economist on the staff of the Joint Economic Committee of Congress. This Congressional unit has long been vocal in its support of a still wider federal economic role, not only with regard to regulating wage levels but in areas ranging from monetary policy to long-range planning. Typical of the Joint Economic Committee's approach is a 1967 proposal urging sharply increased federal spending. "To reach and sustain an economic pattern designed to restore relatively full employment during the next five years," a JEC statement warned, will "require, among other things, a strongly supportive fiscal policy."

Milton Friedman, noting today's huge federal payroll, points to one large reason for the pattern of inexorable governmental growth. "People hired by government know who is their benefactor," he declares. "People who lose their jobs or fail to get them because of [some] governmental program [such as the minimum-wage program] do not know that that is a source of their problem. The good effects are visible. The bad effects are invisible. The good effects generate votes. The bad effects generate discontent, which is as likely to be directed at private business as at the government." He argues that the "great political challenge" of today is "to overcome this bias which has been taking us down the slippery slope to ever bigger government and to the destruction of a free society."

Another eminent economist, Hans F. Sennholz, who heads the economics department at Pennsylvania's Grove City College, is particularly concerned that further governmental growth is all but inevitable as a result of the large, proliferating number of Americans receiving "transfer payments"—federal money, ranging from welfare to Social Security, paid not according to work currently rendered but according to need. Mr. Sennholz notes that some 40 percent of the U.S. population now are "transfer beneficiaries" of one sort or another. "Such programs as Social Security, Medicare, antipoverty, housing and aid-to-education are so popular that few politicians dare oppose them," Mr. Sennholz maintains. He warns: "To reverse the trend and reduce the role of government in our lives, and thus alleviate [government-caused] inflation pressures, is a giant educational task. The social and economic ideas that gave birth to the transfer system must be discredited and replaced with old values of individual independence and self-reliance. The social philosophy of individual freedom and unhampered private initiative must be our guiding light."

The "educating task" that Mr. Sennholz discusses, of course, requires a good deal more than simply altering long-standing attitudes of many politicians and influential bureaucrats. There is the matter of the press, whose members more often than not tend toward a skepticism far more severe when private business practices are in question than when a new governmental program is under scrutiny. There is the matter of the American educational process, where teachers of all levels appear with disturbing frequency to foster kinder attitudes toward officialdom than toward private business. And there is the powerful influence of organized labor, an influence that will be discussed in detail in the next chapter.

* * *

Suffice it here to remark briefly on the matter of the press. A comprehensive study of governmental programs was conducted several years ago by Donald Lambro, a young Washington-based reporter for United Press International. In a book titled *The Federal Rat Hole,* Mr. Lambro cited some 1,000 areas of federal activity that, he had become convinced, should be abandoned. The programs he dissected, by no means a complete list of such federal undertakings, cost taxpayers some $25 billion annually—and, we should add, that figure has risen considerably since Mr. Lambro's book appeared in mid-1975.

In the course of his extensive report, Mr. Lambro attempts to show why he deems all of these projects extravagant, unnecessary and, in many instances, even absurd. And, in the process, he tries to analyze precisely why such programs have met with so little public resistance over the years. He cites many considerations. However, since he happens to be a news-service reporter himself, his discussion of the general attitude of the press, as a factor, is particularly noteworthy. He declares that there has "been too great a tendency within the media to focus on social problems [such as the high jobless rate] while looking to Washington as the pre-eminent solution to those problems. Journalists have all but ignored vast waste in government, which is often as much a burden to taxpayers as some of the very social and economic ills that have consumed the media's attention." Mr. Lambro goes on to note that "occasionally a Congressional committee will focus on some eyesore of government waste needing reform and the media will duly report the event, yet little independent aggressive probing into waste and duplication has been evident." He concludes that the press "tend to think too much in terms of exploring new government programs—as does Congress—and never in terms of exploring whether old ones should be abolished."

* * *

Allen H. Meltzer, the economist at Carnegie-Mellon University, recently issued a study titled "Why Government

Grows." He did not mention a lack of skepticism among press people about new federal programs, nor did he discuss Mr. Nader, his cohorts or the Joint Economic Committee. But he did touch on matters that help to explain such attitudes. "The government grows," he states, "as a result of rational behavior. Individuals and groups concerned with their own interests seek benefits. The [economic] loss that many experience from the continued growth of government does not produce a winning coalition that gains from reducing the size of government." However, the economist stresses, each time a political candidate opposes a program—that is, moves to trim back the governmental economic presence—voters who benefit from the program have a clear incentive to vote against the candidate. Since the benefits of opposing a program will likely not be dramatic and immediate, Mr. Meltzer continues, "fewer voters will be gained than lost."

Mr. Meltzer has no illusions about the difficulties involved in any effort to reverse the growth of the governmental role within the economy. "More votes are gained by promising to increase benefits selectively than by reducing taxes generally or by eliminating programs," he states. "No party or coalition can remain in power permanently, but each party can expect that opponents will use their power to gain selective benefits."

Nonetheless, the Carnegie-Mellon professor concludes that a reversal of the pattern of a growing governmental presence is not impossible. Moreover, in view of the government's distressing impact on both the labor and price fronts, he deems a reversal of the trend has become essential if the economy is to regain vigor. "Nothing about the process is inevitable," according to the professor. "The growth of government could be brought to an end by constitutional limitation. That a limitation of this kind has not been posed, here or elsewhere, may tell a great deal about the cost of persuading, organizing, leading, and maintaining a group large enough to accomplish that goal."

* * *

Any successful effort to deal with the government's growing economic role should begin by dealing with the erroneous notion that central federal planning can lead to a healthier business climate. There is a widespread notion that much of today's economic trouble—the high rates of inflation and unemployment—reflects a lack of governmental planning. At a glance, the notion seems to have some merit. For example, several years ago Senators Hubert Humphrey of Minnesota and Jacob Javits of New York proposed new legislation that would set up an economic planning board within the White House. The idea was that the board would manage to guide the economy's progress with a greater wisdom than is possible with extensive decision-making kept within private-sector hands. At bottom, the proposal reflected a conviction that Washington bureaucrats were best equipped to manage the economy, notwithstanding its awesome diversity.

In 1977, Senator Humphery expressed a concern that most economic planning in the U.S. "is done by private corporations." He went on to bemoan that "there is little coordination among the many independent private planning efforts" and that "government planning is rudimentary and fragmented." He concluded that federally managed economic planning seems a most desirable way to move toward the "nation's goals" of price stability and full employment.

Some prominent members of the academic community share such a sanguine view of planning. An example is

Robert L. Heilbroner, the economic historian and a professor at New York's New School For Social Research. Writing in *The New York Times* in 1976, this economist forecast that "within five years, perhaps much sooner, we will be officially embarked on something called National Economic Planning." He maintained, quite simply, that "if one has faith that a democracy can govern itself, there is no reason to believe that it cannot plan for itself." He wrote glowingly of how officials, working with more accurate, more comprehensive economic statistics, should be able to make wise use of so-called input-output formulas developed by such economists as Wassily Leontief. Through such "flow-chart" techniques, Mr. Heilbroner claimed, federal planners would readily be able to determine, for example, "how much steel, rubber, copper, cloth, etc., it takes to 'cook' an automobile, a steel girder or a billion dollars worth of GNP of a given kind."

In sum, the professor stated, "I envisage the planning process as closely resembling the legislative process." Of the marketplace's role, he had this to add: "The flow of goods from plant to plant or from plant to customer, the entry of labor and capital into industries or their exit from those industries, the organization of production will all be largely entrusted to the profit-seeking, competitive ways of the accustomed market mechanism." However, he quickly went on: "Planning may have to intervene in nonmarket ways, such as by control over prices and wages or by direct materials allocation—but only if milder techniques for controlling inflation or output are ineffective."

Planning, the economist conceded, is "no panacea." It would be foolish, he warned, "to deny that planning carries great risks, including that of a grave restriction of freedom as a consequence of a reckless proliferation of controls."

Nonetheless, he appeared convinced, all things considered, that "in the end, . . . planning offers hope" that the country's troubled economy cannot find elsewhere.

Powerful figures within the Carter Administration from time to time have espoused the alleged virtues of planning. A prime example is Ray Marshall, the President's Labor Secretary. Noting the twin problems of joblessness and unemployment, Mr. Marshall once cautioned that "without planning these trends are likely to continue." He went on to argue that "one of the basic problems we have is unregulated and unplanned market forces."

Labor union leaders also are frequent proponents of a federally planned economy. For example, Leonard Woodcock, long a president of the powerful United Automobile Workers, bluntly says: "Let's face it: we don't live in a small laissez-faire economy anymore; we live in a large, complex, technological society in which planlessness means mass dislocations."

Inadvertently, Mr. Woodcock touches on the very reason that planning cannot lead the way to a vigorous economic environment. He says that today's U.S. economy is large, complex and technological. And so, indeed, it is. But that is all the more reason to eschew governmental planning as any sort of a solution to the country's economic dilemma.

* * *

To understand the fallacy overlooked by such advocates of planning as Mr. Woodcock, a good place to begin is with Friedrich A. Hayek, the Austrian Noble-laureate in economics. Mr. Hayek's book, *The Road to Serfdom,* examines the wide-ranging risks entailed in centralized planning. He elaborated on these ideas in an essay published in 1976 by

Morgan Guaranty Trust. Mr. Hayek refers specifically, in the course of the essay, to Mr. Woodcock. The union leader, he states, "is not, of course, a professional economist and has publicly acknowledged that he did not start to think seriously about economic planning on the part of government" until 1973. Indeed, Mr. Hayek continues, "some of the comments he has made rather suggest that he has not thought much about it."

The crux of Mr. Hayek's objection to the idea of central governmental planning for the economy is spelled out in his Morgan Guaranty essay: "The chief reason why we cannot hope by central direction to achieve anything like the efficiency in the use of resources which the market makes possible is that the economic order of any large society rests on a utilization of the knowledge of particular circumstances widely dispersed among thousands or millions of individuals."

Mr. Hayek argues with conviction that "the alternative of having all the individual managers of businesses convey to a central planning authority the knowledge of particular facts which they possess is clearly impossible—simply because they can never know beforehand which of the many concrete circumstances about which they have knowledge or could find out might be of importance to the central planning authority."

The Noble-laureate proceeds to underscore precisely why the economic complexity concerning Mr. Woodcock and others is the very reason to eschew central planning. "The very complexity which the structure of the modern economic system has assumed provides the strongest argument against central planning," says Mr. Hayek.

> It is becoming progressively less and less imaginable that any one mind or planning authority could possibly survey the millions of connections between the ever more numerous interlocking separate activities which have become indispensable for the efficient use of modern technology and even the maintenance of the standard of life Western man has achieved. That we have been able to achieve a reasonably high degree of order in our economic lives despite modern complexities is only because our affairs have been guided, not by central direction, but by the operations of the market and competition in securing the mutual adjustment of separate efforts.

Is it really seriously contended, Mr. Hayek asks, that some governmental agency—or worse, some politically sensitive plan-making committee—would be more likely to foresee correctly the effects of future changes in tastes, the success of some new device or changes in the scarcity of different raw materials than the producers or professional dealers of these things? Is it really likely, he asks, that a National Planning Office would have a better judgment of the number of cars, generators or frozen foods that we are likely to require five years hence than, say, Ford, General Electric or General Foods?

Mr. Hayek, in passing, gives short shrift to the input-output techniques of Professor Leontief that Robert Heilbroner finds so useful. They may, Mr. Hayek says, "show in an instructive manner how, during some period in the past, various quantities of the products of different main branches of productive activity were used up by other branches." However, he cautions that "how the production of the tens of thousands of different things . . . is determined by the market process is a matter of infinite complexity" that an input-output process cannot possibly pin down.

Not surprisingly, Mr. Hayek views the aforementioned Humphrey-Javits plan as "a decidedly dubious product." Indeed, he concludes that "the whole idea of 'guiding' private industry by announcing beforehand what quantities of different goods firms ought to produce over a long period of the future is a muddle from beginning to end, wholly inefficient [and] destructive of the competitive market and free enterprise and leading by its inherent logic straight to a socialist system."

* * *

Another aspect of the problem with planning was driven home to me several years ago. In 1966, I wrote an article in *The Wall Street Journal* summarizing the views of many economists specializing in providing particularly long-range forecasts of future business developments. Such long-range forecasts, of course, would be particularly useful in any major governmental planning effort to set up centralized economic planning.

It has been unkindly observed from time to time that there is nothing older than yesterday's newspaper. Whether that is true or not, it is a fact that journalists tend only infrequently to check back over the prescience, or lack of prescience, contained in past stories that they have written. In any event, in 1976, I checked back over my 1966 report on how long-range forecasters viewed the economic future. I was aware that many facets of economic activity had not behaved as anticipated by the experts in 1966. And I wanted to sample their views about the post-1976 outlook. I began by contacting a group in Washington that had been especially helpful in

1966, appropriately named the National Planning Association. I approached their chief economic forecaster, Mark Kendall, and that was as far as I got. At the outset, Mr. Kendall, a congenial gentleman not given to abruptness, bluntly told me that he had not recently worked up any long-range forecast. "There is not much interest in long-range forecasts around here anymore," he said, adding with remarkable candor: "We've been wrong too often."

In 1966, NPA forecasters foresaw gross national product in the year 2000 at $2,280 billion, in terms of the 1960 price level. In 1976, a similar long-range forecast compiled by the Commerce Department came up with a comparable GNP figure of only $2,103 billion, nearly $180 billion under the 1966 forecast. It is not necessary to elaborate here the various considerations entering into such altered predictions; suffice it to mention as a major factor a sharply reduced birth rate. The overriding message is that long-range forecasting is a most hazardous game, and this makes the entire planning idea still more dubious. What will the forecasters—those still so bold as to venture out—be saying about the 2000 GNP in 1986? In 1996? Maybe by 1999 they will be getting close to what actually materializes in 2000.

* * *

Warren Nutter, a professor of economics at the University of Virginia, has also served at a high level where the idea of central planning has lots of proponents—in Washington. Drawing upon his experiences as a top official in the Defense Department, Mr. Nutter has this to say about the planning idea: "The movement for planning has a disturbing air about it: the air of reckless experimentation. Look at the mess our economy is in, advocates of planning say. We have tried a lot of things but not central economic planning. Why not give it a try and see what happens? Never mind that it hasn't worked anywhere else: Americans have a way of getting things done."

The economics professor wonders: "Why then did we get into this mess in the first place?" Mr. Nutter answers his own question as follows: "The fact is that we already have the best system of democratic planning there is—the market economy based on private enterprise. Ours is easily the strongest, healthiest, wealthiest, most responsive economy on this planet. The serious economic pains now being experienced are symptoms of political ills, not of flaws in the economic system. The basic problem is too much government, not too little."

* * *

The complaint that the federal government, contrary to a popular view, has lately been too much with us for the good of the economy surfaces again and again among analysts who have devoted long, serious consideration to the inflation-unemployment dilemma. This view, of course, is precisely opposite to the notion that the federal government, above all other institutions, must ultimately lead us out of the dilemma.

Milton Friedman, for example, maintains that governmental measures aimed over the years at reducing inflation and joblessness have in fact "hampered, not helped" the attainment of that economic goal. Indeed, he charges that "the greater part of new ventures undertaken by government in the past few decades have failed to achieve their objectives."

Tilford Gaines of Manufacturers Hanover provides a general description of ways in which misconceived governmental endeavors tend to aggravate inflation and unemployment.

What creates inflation? he asks. A broad answer, he continues, "is misdirected fiscal and monetary policy that, through budget deficits underwritten by the Federal Reserve, creates demands for goods and services without at the same time adding to the supply of these goods and services." Moreover, he observes that the tendency toward inflation "resulting from these practices is complemented by public attitudes toward business that discourage new investments needed to meet growing demand."

Regarding the dilemma's other horn, the economist stresses that business investment spending "has been the principal independent force in promoting . . . employment." To the extent that such investment has been discouraged, he argues, national joblessness has been aggravated.

* * *

A study conducted by Hudson Institute Europe, a Paris-based affiliate of the U.S. "think tank" headed by Herman Kahn, sheds a good deal of light on the connection between governmental activity and economic prosperity. It compares the annual rate of economic growth and the level of governmental spending in 14 countries. The essential finding is that the larger the governmental outlays, the slower the growth. Leading the list, in terms of spending, is Sweden, where governmental outlays amount to about 26 percent of disposable income. Yet, over a 10-year period, Sweden's economic growth averaged only about three percent annually. At the other extreme, such spending in Japan amounts to only 11 percent of income, while Japanese economic growth averaged about 10 percent annually during the 10-year period. Countries where governmental outlays exceed the 20 percent level include, besides Sweden, Denmark, the U.S. and Britain. In all instances, 10-year growth averaged under five percent annually. Countries where the spending rate is below 15 percent include, besides Japan, Australia, France and Spain. In every instance, the Hudson study finds that yearly growth exceeded the five percent level.

Hudson researchers formulate precise estimates of the degree to which the various economies have apparently been hampered by an excessive governmental presence. They find, for example, that in Denmark and Sweden the attainable growth rate was cut by excessive governmental spending by 1.3 to 1.5 percentage points. The comparable reduction in Britain works out to nearly one percentage point. In all, the study suggests, as a rule of thumb, that for each five percent increase in the share of disposable income absorbed by the government there is a one percentage point drop in the growth rate.

It is possible, quite apart from such analyses as the Hudson study, to pinpoint ways in which governmental activity fosters inflation, unemployment and, ultimately, lackluster economic growth. So clear has this governmental aggravation grown that even observers deemed sympathetic to an expanding federal presence have begun expressing doubts.

Hark, for example, to Assar Lindbeck, an eminent Swedish economist whose politican stance in the past marked him a Social Democrat. He recently complained to an interviewer about what he termed the "Swedish sickness." He maintained that his country's economy had suffered extensively as a direct consequence of "the welfare state, with its social benefits" and he implied that the U.S., if recent trends were to persist, faced a similar problem. He decried a system in Sweden where marginal rates of taxation for the average worker, with yearly earnings of roughly $12,000, exceed the 70 percent level.

A similarly jaundiced view of the governmental role was recently provided by a U.S. union leader, Joseph Trerotola, president of Council 16 of the International Brotherhood of Teamsters, Chauffeurs, Warehousemen and Helpers of America. After first complaining that "state and local government taxing policies can and do nullify private-sector union power," the union chieftain continued:

> What government extracts from the individual employer [in taxes] irrevocably reduces the amount of money that employees of that employer will be able to secure through union collective bargaining or individual negotiation. What government extracts in the form of open and concealed taxes from the individual worker simply reduces the amount of money available to the family for food, clothing and shelter. Having only one source to turn to, the worker attempts to replace the monies expropriated by government by escalating his wage demands on the employer. Thus begins the chain reaction which frequently leads to reduced employment opportunities.

It may seem strange to hear a union head sounding like a conservative businessman, charging that big government reduces employment. Mr. Trerotola goes even further. "The tax collector does not pay union dues, does not walk the picket line, but is nevertheless the first beneficiary of any wage increase secured by the worker," he declares, adding: "This perfect stranger gets his cut first, leaving a substantially reduced amount for the family."

* * *

It is impossible to document all the countless ways in which the government's growing presence aggravates the American economic dilemma. A few are painfully apparent. There is, for example, the inflationary impact of the various forms of governmental intervention in the marketplace.

"Government intervention in business has reached the danger point," declares a study by the Conference Board, the nonprofit research group. Surveying 86 business leaders, the Conference Board finds that "there is a widesperad agreement that various government controls are needed to deal with broad economic and social problems . . . but there is a rising criticism over the proliferation of controls and the manner in which they are administered." It concludes: "Discontent is now widespread" abroad as well as in the U.S. The study lists ways in which governmental intervention is deemed to inhibit economic progress—in effect, aggravating both inflation and joblessness. They range from statutory wage increases to the aforementioned rent controls in New York City.

A brief review of the federal regulatory machinery sketches the dimensions of governmental intervention in today's economy.

Federal regulatory agencies are often called the fourth branch of government. Regulations that these agencies issue govern virtually all aspects of economic activity, from the sort of houses we live in to the sort of clothes we wear to the sort of cars we drive to the sort of food we eat. In all, some 50 agencies are involved, employing approximately 100,000 bureaucrats. In 1977, Uncle Sam spent approximately $3.5 billion to carry out various regulatory programs. The largest agency is the Environmental Protection Agency, with some

12,000 employees. Other major ones include the Federal Communications Commission, whose seven commissioners license radio and television stations and oversee telephone and telegraph operations; the Federal Power Commission, whose five commissioners set rates for the interstate transportation and sale of natural gas and electricity; the Civil Aeronautics Board, whose five commissioners decide on interstate airline routes, fares and freight rates; the Securities and Exchange Commission, whose five commissioners regulate the issuing of securities and supervise stock exchanges; the Federal Reserve Board, whose seven members regulate commercial-bank operations and set monetary and credit policy for the nation as a whole; the Equal Employment Opportunity Commission, whose five commissioners rule on charges of racial and other discrimination; the Food and Drug Administration, which, through a commissioner in the Department of Health, Education and Welfare, sets standards for food and drugs; the Federal Trade Commission, whose five commissioners enforce antitrust laws and regulate various business procedures; the Interstate Commerce Commission, whose 11 commissioners set rates and routes for trucks, railroads, buses and pipelines; the Consumer Product Safety Commission, whose five commissioners set product safety standards and send out recall notices on products deemed faulty; and the Federal Aviation Administration, which, through an administrator in the Department of Transportation, checks the safety of aircraft, licenses pilots and sets airport standards. To this long list must be added, of course, the various regulatory operations of the new Department of Energy.

It has been estimated that if all the basic regulations of

these agencies were bound together, a 60,000-page book would be the result. It would occupy a shelf more than 15 feet long.

* * *

Besides all this federal regulatory activity, of course, there is the rapidly expanding regulatory role of states and other nonfederal governmental units. A glance at just one facet of nonfederal regulation—in the area of licensing—gives an indication of this pervasive, often oppressive form of governmental intervention in the marketplace. It is estimated that the various states now require licenses in about 500 occupations. In some states, licensed employees in private businesses approximate one-fourth of the work force. Occupations requiring a license in various states range from fish-bait dealers to wig stylists.

Various studies show that spreading state licensing is contributing to both inflation and unemployment, and, in addition, often entails other serious problems. Economists at the University of Tennessee recently analyzed 31 licensed occupations and found that "the more stringent the licensing requirements, the lower the quantity and quality of the services consumers received." They explain that licensing tends to increase costs for consumers and often forces low-income consumers to rely on unlicensed "quacks." Another finding: excessive licensing prompts dangerous do-it-yourself efforts. For instance, the study reports a connection between areas where electricians must be strictly licensed—such as Vermont—and accidental electrocutions of do-it-yourselfers.

* * *

It is impossible to put an inflationary price tag, or an added-unemployment figure, on the impact of governmental interference in the marketplace. No one can reasonably argue against a minimum level of governmental regulation—for example, of food and medicine products and of pollution standards. But, as we have seen, the governmental hand now extends far beyond such necessary areas. President Ford in 1975 placed the annual cost of "wasteful and unnecessary" governmental intervention in the marketplace at roughly $2,000 per American family. Murray L. Weidenbaum, a former official in the Treasury Department who now teaches economics at Washington University in St. Louis, estimates that the "rising array of government regulations," many of them unnecessary, add between $1,500 and $2,500 to the price of a new house. My own recent experience is that Mr. Weidenbaum may be conservative in this regard. I was recently compelled by local regulations to install five cesspools plus a septic tank—far more than I could possibly ever use—near the site of a not-large house that I recently built in the New York area. Three cesspools would have been more than adequate, but regulations specified a minimum of five.

"The litany of regulatory absurdities is long and continues to grow," Secretary of Commerce Juanita M. Kreps conceded in a 1977 speech before a meeting of top business executives. She proceeded to tick off a list of "inanities." Among those she noted:

> Today truckers may go from Baltimore to Albany and from Albany to Boston. The truckers are not permitted to go directly from Baltimore to Boston unless the distance savings is less than 20 percent. You heard me correctly; I

said unless the savings is less than 20 percent. With an energy shortage staring us in the face, how much sense does that make?

The steel industry for years has been struggling to compete with stiff foreign competition. What have we asked them to do? We have asked them to comply with 5,600 separate regulations imposed by some 27 different governmental agencies. The cost of simply determining what compliance requires is staggering.

The consumer product safety commission classifies auto batteries as household items, and requires manufacturers to attach a label to each battery warning the public not to drink its contents. This regulation cost consumers $5,000,000 in 1975.

Dow Chemical wanted to build a $500,000,000 petrochemical plant in California. To do this, Dow had to obtain 68 permits, approvals, and leases from more than a dozen local, regional, state and federal agencies. After two years of delays and $4,000,000 spent to comply with environmental regulations and government red tape, Dow had only received four permits. They decided to discontinue the project. As a result, 1,000 permanent jobs will not be created in an area which already has substantial unemployment.

Misguided federal programs are a painful manifestation of the distress that can result from governmental involvement in the marketplace. Elizabeth Holtzman, a New York City congresswoman, has been particularly critical, for example, of federally financed summer-job programs in her city. The programs are designed to help youngsters gain skills to make them more employable. Miss Holtzman concluded after a close look at the progress of the federal effort that the programs were actually making participating youngsters "less employable." Officials running the programs, she said, tolerated absenteeism and tardiness and refused to invoke any sort of discipline aimed at instilling good work habits. She called the entire undertaking "absolutely intolerable and disgraceful and inexcusable."

Other, larger instances of misguided federal endeavors abound. The Commerce Department reckons that only about 35 percent of money spent on construction projects actually winds up as wages in workers' pockets. It has been estimated, along the same line, that $2 billion spent in public-works grants in 1976, for instance, created only 80,000 jobs.

It hardly bears emphasizing that such activity is highly conducive to accelerating inflation. It should be added that much of the misguided federal largess is well nigh uncontrollable. A study by the Office of Management and Budget, which the ill-fated Bert Lance headed briefly at the start of the Carter Administration, estimates that some 72 percent of the $324.6 billion spent by the government in a recent 12 months was "relatively uncontrollable." These spending items that were largely immune to any budget-cutting ax included Social Security outlays, interest on the federal debt, unemployment assistance, veterans' benefits and revenue-sharing with states.

* * *

Uncontrollable spending notwithstanding, it is disturbingly clear that some effort to roll back the governmental presence is essential if Americans are to begin to deal with the dilemma besetting the U.S. economy.

This would be no simple undertaking. Certainly, recent

U.S. history suggests a continuing trend in the opposite direction of increasing governmental involvement. Yet, here and there, encouraging signs of a new awareness are emerging. The aforementioned speech by Commerce Secretary Juanita Kreps is an illustration of change. She is, after all, a cabinet officer in an administration representing the political party usually associated with more, rather than less, governmental activity. Yet, she is highly critical of governmental "inanities." Her speech, indeed, does more than list just a few examples of the economic harm big government can inflict. "What can be done?" she asks, and then proceeds to mention several recent steps that have been taken. One is the Carter Administration's move to eliminate "regulations that raise prices and block competition." She notes the administration's 1977 decision to overrule the Civil Aeronautics Board and allow U.S. carriers to offer flights to London competitive with the cheapest charter offerings. She notes that "the Labor Department has for months been hard at work pruning the Occupational Safety and Health Administration's regulations." Other agencies attempting to reduce "conflicts" between their rules and the economic activity among businesses that they regulate, according to Mrs. Kreps, include the Interstate Commerce Commission, the Environmental Protection Agency, the Food and Drug Administration and the Consumer Product Safety Commission.

In the talk, Mrs. Kreps goes on to note that some regulatory agencies "are cliches of Congress and [are] beholden largely to Congress." Accordingly, she warns that there are limits to the amount of regulatory reform that President Carter or any other chief executive can achieve. "Many businesses' regulatory problems will have to be solved in the same form in which they were created, in Congress," she concedes.

To spur Congressional reform, she urges Congressional passage of so-called sunset legislation under which all regulations would automatically cease to exist after a specified number of years, unless their continuation were specifically authorized by Congress after careful assessment.

The need for Congressional action was foreseen by President Ford in his 1977 State of the Union Address. "We have made some progress in cutting back the expansion of government and its intrusion into individual lives," he stated, but "believe me, there is much more to be done by tough and temporarily painful surgery by a Congress as prepared as the President to face up to this very real political problem."

* * *

There are signs, as well, that business executives are beginning to understand their responsibilities in any effort to roll back governmental involvement in the economy. The Conference Board survey that found increasing executive concern about the government's role in economic affairs also found that "companies are intensifying their efforts . . . to reverse the trend." It reported that "a growing number of firms are encouraging their officers and employees to play more active roles in trade associations which present business views to government, supporting research projects which create and promote alternatives to present governmental programs, and establishing a variety of political-action groups."

This executive attitude is evident in a talk delivered by Walter B. Wriston, chairman of Citicorp. "For all their insight," he said, "the framers of our Constitution could not foresee a day when approximately 500 legislators would employ 10,000 people to assist them in their legislative tasks.

But they could have told their modern successors that such a horde would propose far too much legislation." In 1976, he added, "there were 20,000 bills introduced in Congress in a single day, and not less than 242 committees and subcommittees of the Congress were in session—all, under the rules, for a legislative purpose."

What can be done? the banker asks. His solution sounds remarkably similar to the "sunset" legislation urged by Mrs. Kreps: "It is time to call for the majority of laws to expire by their own terms." And he offers another proposal: "Let us have a constitutional amendment that would limit the Congressional session to six or seven months; Parkinson's Law would still work, but with a little luck we can cut down the number of new laws." Parkinson's "Second Law," of course, states that "work expands to fill the time available."

Another articulate executive who has been long urging a concerted effort to trim the government's economic role is Roger M. Blough, a former chairman of United States Steel Corp. He readily concedes that the government's "regulatory mill grinds on." But he urges that the matter not be left to rest there. "Faith in Washington problem-solving is faltering," he says. Among steps that he urges are an end to various governmental restrictions on the interstate movement of agricultural products, more freedom for banks to compete with one another and pay interest to depositors as they see fit, and fewer restrictions on competition between various forms of transportation. President Carter's move to allow more competitive air fares is clearly a step along this line.

An indication that President Carter may be increasingly aware of the economic peril posed by excessive regulation can be found in the Federal Register. An unusually straightforward passage in the massive federal rule book states, quite simply, that "regulations should be as simple and clear as possible. They should achieve legislative goals effectively and efficiently. They should not impose unnecessary burdens on the economy, on individuals, on public or private organizations, or on state and local governments."

* * *

A measure that has gained increasing support as a means of limiting the inflationary impact of excessive federal spending involves indexing tax rates. James W. Fella, an economist at Celanese Corp., explains that "the government does not have incentive to change the tax structure, or to wage an all-out war on inflation because the higher the inflation, the more taxes it collects, the more it has available to spend or pay off old debts." The economist argues that "if inflation cannot be stopped in the short term, its impact on taxes would be" stopped by a program of adjusting individual tax rates to allow for inflation. A person's tax bracket would be automatically changed according to the annual rate of inflation, as well as any salary change. Tax payments as a percentage of income would increase only when a worker's spending power—the actual purchasing power of the paycheck—increased. A *Fortune* magazine editorial, titled "Some Prescriptions for Government Bloat," argues, similarly, that "the continuation of inflation and the progressive income tax make things easier for benefit-bestowing politicians." In effect, it observes, the "government rakes in extra revenue without having to raise tax rates," always a painful step for politicians.

Perhaps the most difficult task in curbing inflationary government "bloat," as *Fortune* puts it, is dealing with the "uncontrollable" items that soak up taxpayer revenues and keep budgetary red ink flowing massively. For the most part, as we have seen, these entail automatic transfers of funds to anyone eligible under various entitlement formulas. Such payments, at about $12 billion annually in the mid-1950's, now approximate $200 billion. Outlays for a dozen key uncontrollable items are projected to exceed $309 billion by early in the next decade.

The great difficulty in coping with such mushrooming growth is that new legislation is needed, in the main, to correct the situation. A surprising Congressional willingness to take painful steps to improve the financial health of the troubled Social Security program—one of the dozen noted above—may be a sign of a new Congressional toughness. New Congressional budget-making machinery may be another. However, the unhappy fact is that many lawmaking politicians are stubbornly reluctant to acknowledge the economic harm that is clearly stemming from the government's enormous growth. The solution lies, to a large extent, in a more enlightened Congress. That may come if more people like Juanita Kreps and Walter Wriston and even Jimmy Carter begin to speak out about the harm, as well as the much-publicized good, that a massive governmental presence can cause the economy.

CHAPTER ELEVEN

Dealing with Labor

It is somewhat ironic that the word "labor" is often taken nowadays to mean labor unions. For union members constitute, as we will see, only a relatively minor fraction of the American labor force. But it is an undeniably important fraction whose influence is felt right across America's diverse labor scene—the unorganized areas as well as the organized.

There is no question that the unemployment-inflation bind gripping the U.S. economy derives in part from developments arising on the labor front. And there can be no doubt that any reasonable discussion of unemployment and inflation necessitates an extensive look at the role of labor, particularly organized labor. Indeed, any lasting solution to the country's economic dilemma requires dealing with longstanding labor-force patterns. Because these patterns generally emerge most clearly within labor's organized sector, much of this chapter's discussion will center there. Although they are in the minority, unionized workers unmistakably set the trend in a national work force that will soon be moving above the 100 million mark.

Few observers would dispute the need of many categories

of workers to organize themselves. Without unions, people in all sorts of occupations would surely be subjected to a variety of employer abuse. Unionization, on balance, has proved highly beneficial to the country's economic development over many decades. Still, in recent years it has become increasingly evident that in certain ways organized labor is tending to aggravate both unemployment and inflation.

For years, of course, business executives have maintained that unions, with their strike power, are a major reason for persistent inflation. The argument has been that, with their perfectly legal ability to shut down their employers' facilities, unions continually are able to extract excessive pay increases from management. These increases, the argument runs, generally far exceed increases in worker productivity, with the result—discussed in detail in Chapter Seven—that per-unit labor costs shoot up. To prevent operating at a loss, the company in question moves to offset the labor-cost jump by raising prices.

Undeniably, there is some validity to this contention. The law does indeed provide unionized labor with a degree of muscle at the bargaining table that seems in some respects unfair—and inflation-producing. Yet, this does not excuse countless instances where, for example, the management side may have been too quick to grant labor demands. After all, notwithstanding union clout, a process of negotiation does still exist. Employers can hardly be viewed as blameless in the upward spiral of labor costs that has marked the last decade or so.

* * *

Whatever the precise degree of union responsibility for today's inflation, unemployment is perhaps the area where organized labor's influence is most pernicious and, strangely, least recognized. Dealing with unemployment necessitates a recognition of this fact. It means dealing with a union influence which, for all its virtues, clearly limits the economy's considerable capacity to provide jobs for a citizenry whose inclination to work, happily, seems well nigh insatiable.

The task of dealing with this problem is made doubly difficult by a general, and no doubt genuine, unawareness. Union leaders, for example, do not hesitate to underscore the painful aspects of unemployment. This emphasis can be seen in a statement issued by George Meany of the AFL-CIO in 1975, near the pit of the 1973-75 recession. A typical passage:

> Recession is the greatest waste of all. It cost 25 million American jobs in the last 25 years. Do you know that 25 million people have been laid off because of the recession? It has cost us $300 billion in lost incomes in two years. And this recession, according to the government's statistics, will cost the American economy $1.5 trillion between now and 1980. Just like you went to the toilet and flushed it and threw it down into the sewer.

Another Meany statement, issued several months later, shows plainly the union leader's admirable concern over the social damage caused by persistent joblessness. An example:

> High unemployment also affects the way a society perceives itself. The longer people are out of work, the more desperate their situation becomes. Yet the longer people are unemployed, the easier it is for the well off and the comfortable to ignore the human problems caused by joblessness. . . . High unemployment also creates stresses and strains within society, further widening the gap between

the haves and the have nots; pitting worker against worker for the available work; creating division where there should be unity. Just as America could not survive as a nation that segregated its races, it cannot survive if it segregates its people between those who work and those who are always jobless.

There is absolutely no recognition in any of these statements that organized labor itself has had a very large hand in the country's jobless problem. Rather, the blame is pinned on a political leadership—as it happened, the Ford Administration—which, according to Mr. Meany, stubbornly refused "to take any action designed to put America back to work."

* * *

Before taking a closer look at ways in which organized labor unwittingly tends to aggravate the very unemployment that so concerns Mr. Meany and other leaders, let us glimpse at the somewhat paradoxical position of unions in today's economy. On the one hand, in purely statistical terms, the presence of unions on the national stage has diminished in recent years to a surprising extent. On the other hand, in ways less easily pinpointed, union clout has grown markedly, to a point where it influences all manner of national activity—on the economic front, in foreign policy, in a range of sociological areas.

The diminishing union presence can be traced with a few statistics. In the early 1950's, about 25 percent of the country's labor force was made up of union members. Now, the comparable percentage is roughly 20 percent. The labor force, of course, has grown enormously in the last quarter of a century. In the early 1950's, it amounted to about 70 million persons. Now, it is near the 100 million mark. Thus, in absolute terms, union membership has risen moderately. But the figures make clear that the growth has lagged far behind the overall growth of the labor force. The reasons for this lag are complex and not entirely clear. But one unmistakable factor is that the sort of jobs that have been proliferating most rapidly in recent decades are often in businesses where unionization has traditionally tended to be weak. Service-type jobs—for example, computer programmers and television-repair personnel—are among the employment categories where such growth has occurred. At the same time, job expansion has tended to be minimal in some categories where union strength has long been considerable—for instance, blue-collar employment in industries ranging from steel to automobiles.

Also serving to diminish union representation has been a massive movement of industry into southern regions of the country. Union membership has always lagged in the South. Even now, after considerable union efforts to organize more workers in the South, the percentage of organized workers in state after state remains far below the national average—for instance, seven percent in North Carolina, eight percent in South Carolina, 14 percent in Georgia, 13 percent in Texas and 12 percent in Mississippi and Florida. Comparable percentages for several northern states include 38 percent in Michigan, New York and Pennsylvania, 35 percent in Illinois and 33 percent in Indiana and Ohio. Unlike many northern states, most southern states have so-called right-to-work laws. These laws forbid "union shops," which require union membership as a condition of keeping a job.

Yet, despite the decline in the percentage of union members in the labor force, Roper Reports, which conducts periodic surveys of Americans' attitudes, recently came up with a notable finding. The polling agency asked a cross-section of the citizenry which major national groups seemed to have "too much power and influence." Remarkably, 65 percent of those responding cited labor unions. This was up from 55 percent in a comparable Roper survey four years earlier. It should be added that those viewing big business as wielding too much power declined in the four years to 59 percent from 66 percent. As a result, labor wound up at the top of Roper's "too powerful" list, with business a distant second. This represented a reversal of the situation four years earlier.

* * *

How can this be? If union membership represents a shrinking portion of the labor force, why does the public generally regard organized labor as "too powerful" and growing more so?

Part of the explanation, of course, can be found in the change at the White House, noted in the first chapter. A Republican President, widely regarded at pro-business despite a record of high inflation and deep recession, was replaced by a Democratic President whose support was heavily buttressed by organized labor, particularly by Mr. Meany's AFL-CIO.

Though organized labor may represent a smaller fraction of the labor force nowadays, there is evidence aplenty that its ability to get solidly and effectively behind a political candidate has improved mightily. This can be seen in the political action arm of the AFL-CIO, an organization known as COPE—for Committee on Political Education. A. H. Raskin, a veteran journalist and an authority on labor matters, concluded after the 1976 Presidential election that COPE "far outdistanced the political action groups representing business." R. Heath Larry, chairman of the National Association of Manufacturers, a management-oriented group largely pro-Republican, commented, along the same line, that "we were outclassed" by the union organization. And a representative of the Republican National Committee conceded, at the same time, that COPE "probably made the difference in the Presidential contest." He estimated that COPE spent some $18 million drumming up votes for Jimmy Carter in the election. "When you put that much money on top of the $25 million to which the law limited direct spending by each of the Presidential candidates," he added, "it had to be decisive for Carter."

Regarding such figures, Mr. Larry charged that "a kind of double standard operates when it comes to labor on these off-the-balance-sheet items of money. . . . Business has had to be very cautious on this kind of thing." In the 1972 election, in contrast to the situation in 1976, organized labor, in the words of Mr. Raskin, "was all over the map" when irritation over the Democrats' nomination of Senator George McGovern for the Presidency caused Mr. Meany to declare an AFL-CIO policy of political neutrality. This policy unquestionably helped Richard Nixon in his landslide victory.

Organized labor was definitely not "all over the map" in its role during the 1976 Presidential election. Unlike the 1972 situation, in 1976 the unions generally banded together behind the Carter ticket. "The victory of Carter and his running mate, Minnesota Senator Walter Mondale, culminated 15 weeks of intensive political activity since the AFL-CIO Executive Council endorsed the slate on July 19," declared a report in the *AFL-CIO News,* the labor group's weekly newspaper, just after the 1976 election. It added:

> Labor worked hard for Carter's victory. . . . The importance of the labor effort is emphasized by the fact that the loss of New York's 41 electoral votes would have denied Carter the victory. Carter's final week's visit to New York's garment center gave him the biggest turnout of the campaign. Similar late stops were made by Carter and Mondale to key labor audiences in Pennsylvania, Ohio and Minnesota.

In light of this crucial role in getting Jimmy Carter ensconced in the White House, it is not surprising that organized labor is widely regarded as an increasingly powerful entity. In early 1977, *Business Week* magazine produced an editorial titled "Labor Presents Its Bill." The article noted that "organized labor vigorously backed Jimmy Carter" in the 1976 election and, as a result of his victory, "has lost no time in presenting its bill for services rendered." One item on the list is an extensive overhaul of fundamental labor laws in order, as the editorial put it, "to expedite union organizing." Still another increase in the minimum wage—to $2.65 an hour, effective at the start of 1978—was a part of labor's list which received prompt Presidential and Congressional attention. The insidious effect of minimum-wage regulations on the economy's health was noted in Chapter Three. It is an indication of union clout that such legislation could be pushed so readily through Washington's lawmaking machinery. There can be no question that President Carter and prominent, experienced legislators are well aware that repeated, large increases in the minimum wage tend to aggravate unemployment, particularly among black teen-agers, where the jobless problem is so painful and intractable.

Union clout can also be detected in widespread political

support for legislation mandating governmental economic policies that would, in the words of Vice President Mondale, "put everyone in this country back to work." Such legislation, however impractical and inflation-producing it may be, signifies a very large step beyond 1946 legislation known as the "Full Employment Act." The 1946 law was so vague that it failed to pinpoint its own goals and did not place policymakers under any real pressure to stimulate economic growth. It merely urged them, in effect, to pursue full employment, without defining either the means to be used or the precise goal.

In any event, Vice President Mondale was speaking with utter honesty when he told an AFL-CIO gathering that "we couldn't have won without you." He further pledged that the Carter Administration would "fulfill the trust and the faith that you demonstrated in us" during the 1976 election.

* * *

The political clout of organized labor did not end with the return to power of a Democratic politician in the White House. It continues. An illustration can be found in the *AFL-CIO News*. The publication provides boxscores of how each Congressman and Senator votes on key pieces of legislation. There is nothing subtle about these boxscores. Alongside each legislator's name is a symbol—an *R* or a *W*—indicating for readers whether the individual voted "right" or "wrong" on a particular issue.

A discussion of the expanding clout of organized labor appears in a recent report of the Economic Education and Research Forum, a Chicago-based economic-research service. "One may ask how labor unions have managed to corner so much of the special privilege legislation relative to other pressure groups," the report states. "The answer is relatively simple. They are gaining . . . because of the huge organized voting block they represent." Anyone who works in a non-union capacity at the offices of any large corporation is surely well aware, in contrast, that no such "organized voting block" exists there.

Looking down the road, there is reason to believe that the political clout of unions will continue to expand, notwithstanding the public's increasing criticism that organized labor is becoming "too powerful." The Carter Administration is relatively new, and in any event the Republican opposition seems disorganized for an effective drive on the White House in the next Presidential election. In addition, some observers are convinced that the aforementioned shrinkage of union representation within the labor force may be at or near an end. Efforts to increase unionization throughout the South are well advanced, and they are likely to be abetted by legislation forthcoming from a Washington controlled by the Democratic Party. Already, it is clear that union membership is sharply on the rise in many white-collar occupations where representation heretofore had been lagging. In 1978, the United Steel Workers union still boasted the largest number of members within the AFL-CIO. But the total was about 10 percent lower than in 1975. At the same time, the State, County and Municipal Employees Union, growing swiftly, moved into third place, displacing a blue-collar union representing machinists. Other mainly white-collar unions moving rapidly up the ladder include those representing such employees as retail clerks, public-service workers and communication workers. An example of such white-collar gains by unions can be seen in the following statistics:

In a recent 10 years, the number of state and local workers climbed from 7.2 million to 11.5 million, a rise of about 60 percent; however, in the same interval, the number of union members within those two totals swelled from 1.5 million to 3.9 million, a gain of 160 percent.

The determination of organized labor to gain new members in new areas, previously largely nonunion, is also evident in the AFL-CIO's continuing effort to send trained speakers around to address, without charge, various nonunion organizations. An extreme example was the labor group's recent offer to have its lecturers explain to Chambers of Commerce around the country the details of organized labor's drive to overhaul federal labor law. Although the offer was laudable, the AFL-CIO found no takers among the country's 6,600 local chambers.

* * *

Precisely because the clout of organized labor is so considerable, and likely to continue to increase, it is unfortunate indeed that so much of what the union leadership urges is misguided and downright harmful in many instances to the general health of the economy—including even its unionized elements.

The wrongheadness of the union approach is most plainly apparent, perhaps, in the minimum-wage debate. A trip to Florida brought home to me the full dimensions of this wrongheadness. In early 1977, on a reporting assignment for *The Wall Street Journal,* I traveled to Florida's Dade County area, where unemployment, particularly among black teenagers, happened to be painfully high. The purpose of the trip was to interview black youths and social workers in the area. The idea was to determine what if any impact the prevailing minimum-wage law was having on their employment prospects. The interviews showed a distressing pattern. A survey of some 100 youths found fully 40 percent looking for work without success. The others either held jobs or did not want any. Significantly, nearly half of those looking claimed they would be willing to work for less than the $2.30 an hour that then was the minimum wage. Office work and restaurant jobs were frequently cited as occupations in which minimum-wage rules tended to limit the hiring of youths.

Among the teen-agers surveyed was Maggie Jones, a 17-year-old black. Maggie, who had recently given birth to a boy, was unemployed but wanted work. Guided by Dade County social workers, she had applied for work in enterprises ranging from fast-food chains to department stores. However, she said, the answer that she received was "always no, there's nothing available just now."

Would she work for less than $2.30 an hour? "You bet I would, but there aren't many jobs like that around," she replied.

Jimmy Harris, an 18-year-old black neighbor of Maggie's, also wanted a job. He had had one the previous year, helping with inventories in a department store. It paid $2.30 an hour, and he said he liked it. But he had been laid off the previous Christmas when the pre-Christmas shopping rush subsided. Like Maggie, Jimmy claimed that he would gladly work for less than $2.30 an hour. But "there is nothing around," he said, even though he is a high school graduate.

Leonard Murray, a 17-year-old black, had had job interviews at Miami branches of two fast-food chains, but he said, "I've had no luck." He had earned $2.60 an hour in a metalworking plant; however, he had been recently laid off. "I would have been happy to work there the rest of my life," he said. "It was an eight-hour day, but I really had to work hard only three or four hours." He reckoned that "there would be more work if there was no minimum wage" for teen-agers.

Deborah Evans, 17 and black, earned $15 a week babysitting for a neighbor. The job, which was steady, entailed about four hours of work a day, so that on an hourly basis she received far less than the $2.30 minimum. Neither Deborah nor her neighbor seemed aware that a federal regulation was being violated. Although casual babysitting for a few hours a week isn't subject to minimum-wage rules, Labor Department officials say that a job such as Deborah's, which involved more than 20 hours a week, clearly comes under the regulations.

In any event, Deborah seemed happy with the job. If she were to demand $2.30 an hour, she said, the neighbor simply wouldn't be able to afford her services, the job would "disappear" and the neighbor would either have to give up her own job or leave young children alone in the house.

To try simply to enforce federal minimum-wage regulations, the government employs about 1,000 so-called compliance officers. Complaints from workers also help. In a recent 12-month interval, employers paid nearly $71 million to some 447,000 workers who had been receiving less than federal law required. But no one knows precisely how many violations of minimum-wage regulations go on.

Federal officials say enforcement is difficult and will grow even harder now that the minimum wage has been raised and coverage expanded once again. Over the years, more and more job categories have been coming under the regulations. Recently, for example, the law was extended to more than 500,000 workers in certain types of chain-store outlets.

Betty Jackson gave me a message when I was in Florida

for the people in Washington who wanted to raise the nation's minimum wage:

Drop dead.

If you suspect that Betty Jackson is a profit-greedy employer of unskilled workers who toil in some sweatshop for the minimum wage, you are wrong. Plump, middle-aged, black, the mother of four ranging from 18 years of age down to 12, she employs no one. She is poor, and she herself is employed, at modest pay, as a social worker by Dade County. Her job is to try to find work for jobless teen-agers in a poverty-ridden area just north of Miami. "It would be just awful for the kids if the federal authorities raise the minimum wage again," the black woman told me during my visit. "It's bad enough now, but if the wage floor goes up again, the kids simply won't get hired."

Since Mrs. Jackson told me that, President Carter signed legislation increasing the hourly wage to $2.65 on January 1, 1978, then to $2.90 on January 1, 1979, then to $3.10 on January 1, 1980, and then to $3.35 on January 1, 1981. Congress gave final approval to the plan on October 20, 1977, with a vote of 236 to 187 in the House of Representatives. The Democratic majority there turned aside arguments by Republicans that the wage-floor boosts each year would be inflationary and close thousands of jobs to younger jobseekers. A proposal to allow a split-level minimum, with a lower floor for young workers, was also turned aside. The idea was strongly opposed by organized labor.

When the legislation was enacted, the AFL-CIO hailed it as "a big boost" for the nation's "dragging economy." A less ebullient, but more intelligent, reaction appeared about the same time in a *Business Week* editorial. "All in all," it stated, "Congress in its effort to please organized labor has chosen the worst possible means of dealing with the nation's twin problems of inflation and unemployment. . . . The U.S. will be paying a high price for the labor support that Congressmen have just stockpiled for the next election." It warned that raising the minimum wage would inevitably push the "whole pay structure of U.S. industry upward because unions will insist on maintaining the long-established pay differentials between job categories." And it warned as well that a higher minimum would "destroy jobs that could have been available to marginal workers; unskilled inexperienced workers will not be able to produce enough to justify the cost of hiring them."

Betty Jackson, down in Dade County, does not read *Business Week* editorials. But the concern expressed in that particular editorial could have come right out of her mouth.

* * *

Union wrongheadness is also aggravating unemployment among workers not directly affected by minimum-wage increases.

Keeping up with the minimum wage is not a problem faced by members of building-trades unions across the country. But keeping a job has become the major problem for these AFL-CIO unionists. Over the years, these workers have been enormously successful in using their organized power to boost sharply their hourly wage rates to levels generally more than twice as high as the national average for all workers. In early 1978, as a result of repeated success at the bargaining table, the average hourly pay for a journeyman plumber amounted to $13.71. Other job categories within the building-trades group also boasted exceptionally high hourly pay levels—$13.49 for electricians, $12.71 for bricklayers, $12.54

for carpenters, $11.49 for painters and $9.87 for unskilled laborers.

In view of such statistics, one would presume that this particular segment of organized labor, at the least, would constitute a contented, even jolly crew. But that is hardly the case. Unhappiness abounds. Unemployment among these union members has been running at about twice the national average, or substantially above 10 percent. Moreover, the building-trades unions, long among those most strongly unionized, have been losing many members. Robert A. Georgine, president of the Building and Construction Trades Department of the AFL-CIO, concedes glumly that members by the thousands have recently "put their union cards in their pockets or their shoes and gone to work" in nonunion jobs because, quite simply, they need work. This exodus has occurred, he notes, even though nonunion pay scales range 20 percent to 25 percent below comparable union levels.

In a recent 12 months, construction unions participated in only 226 National Labor Relations Board elections and lost 118 of them. Only 2,637 building tradesmen were organized in the process, a minuscule fraction of the approximately 4 million union people in the construction industry.

"Many tradesmen are laying down their tools and quitting the industry," warns a study prepared by the Building and Construction Trades Department of the AFL-CIO. The analysis, in an effort to draw attention to the group's problems, goes on:

> These workers constitute some of this country's most skilled workers. Many of them have spent up to six years learning their trades. The loss of such valuable human resources and the suffering experienced by the workers and

their families is irreparable. Equally tragic will be the consequences our entire nation faces in the not-so-distant future when we once again begin to face up to our tremendous needs in the area of housing, mass transit, energy supply facilities, and the like. All these projects will require vast numbers of skilled tradesmen, craftsmen who are being driven from the industry and incoming apprentices who are being discouraged from seeking work in the industry.

For many years now, the report adds, "construction's unemployment rate has exceeded that of every other major industry group and has regularly been approximately twice as high as the economy-wide range." It concludes by blaming the gloomy record on such factors as construction activity's particular "sensitivity" to the economy's periodic ups and downs, and the highly seasonal nature of much of the business, particularly in northern parts of the country.

All this may be true. But a significant omission from the list is the fact that the pay levels prevailing among unionized construction workers, after all the years of steep increases, are the envy of the American work force. Nobody envies the group's jobless rate, however. Instead, it stands as a dismal demonstration of the economic damage—in this case involving a loss of jobs—that a shortsighted union leadership can cause.

The sorry record in construction employment merely constitutes an extreme illustration of misguided union policies that aggravate the country's jobless problem. Other examples abound. These range from overly rigid work-rule procedures to overly stringent entrance requirements for union apprentices. The former tend to cause joblessness in export industries, as well as other places, by eroding American competitiveness in world markets. The latter tend to cause unemployment among young persons who, with an adequate apprenticeship, could fill jobs that now go begging because of shortages of special skills.

* * *

Some union policies also serve, quite apparently, to aggravate inflation. Already mentioned is the unfortunate impact of a rapidly climbing minimum wage, heartily endorsed by organized labor, on teen-age employment. In addition, of course, a rising minimum wage tends to push wages higher all along the line, as more senior employees seek to preserve the distance between their own wage levels and those of their less-well-paid confreres. The upshot is a general increase in pay levels, up and down the line. To the extent that employers can pass this increase along to customers, prices will rise and inflation will worsen.

On the international front, as well, policies advocated by union chieftains generally serve to worsen the country's price spiral. Trade protectionism is one such area. The AFL-CIO leadership, for example, has long been plugging for tougher restrictions on imports into the U.S. At its 1977 convention in Los Angeles, the group strongly endorsed a wide range of protectionist measures, including import quotas on some items and higher tariffs on others. Such moves are clearly inflationary to the extent that they keep from American consumers foreign-made products that are cheaper than their U.S.-made counterparts.

In the international arena, organized labor also has long urged that steps be taken to make it more difficult for U.S.-based multinational corporations to set up factories and operate abroad. The idea has been that these "runaway" plants, in effect, rob American labor of jobs that would otherwise be performed in this country. The trouble with the notion is that, in all likelihood, the jobs in any event would not be performed in this country. If a particular U.S. multinational were precluded from setting up a widget factory in, say, France, the chances are that some other multinational, perhaps a West German concern, would step into the void. Unless the economics of the idea were enticing, the U.S.-based firm most likely would still refrain from building a new widget plant in the U.S. In the process, American industry's competitive stance in the international marketplace would suffer. Ultimately, the effect on American consumers would be similar to the effect of import quotas and other such protectionism—to isolate American industry. Such isolation, of course, fosters high-cost, inefficient production procedures. And they, in turn, are a major cause of inflationary pressure within the American economy today.

Organized labor also tends to aggravate the price spiral by its constant urging that the government take stronger steps to speed economic growth. The unions, as noted earlier, profess a deep concern over the nation's unemployment level. And they maintain, accordingly, that the economy must be spurred sharply so that swift growth will bring markedly lower rates of joblessness. Typical of the union drumbeat is a talk given in 1976 by the late Nathaniel Goldfinger, the AFL-CIO's director of research. Although economic growth was accelerating and employment rising sharply at the time of the talk, the union economist declared: "We need a government commitment of full employment, to bring down unemployment fast—as fast as possible, and prevent unemployment from ever again rising above three percent of the labor force." As we have seen, all the evidence of recent years suggests that a riproaring rate of inflation—well up into double digits, at the least—would develop long before Mr. Goldfinger's three percent jobless rate would materialize.

In a similar vein, the sort of monetary and fiscal policy urged by organized labor—extra-rapid growth in the money supply to induce extra-low interest rates and red-ink budgets—also seems a certain prescription for a severe worsening of inflation. Again, union support for a sharply expanded program of public works appears a most inflationary way of trying to create jobs. There is widespread agreement among economists that the public-works route is a particularly costly way to create jobs. For one thing, such jobs generally are of a temporary nature. The individual involved may find himself out on the street again before long. Moreover, it is unlikely that any useful skills will have been acquired that could facilitate reemployment. For another thing, a high degree of inefficiency tends to prevail in the public-works area. Unlike private industry, where managers must try to keep their operations in the black, the administrators of public-works jobs are likely to disregard the private enterprise's famous "bottom line," in the knowledge that governmental rather than private funds are involved. The upshot is a highly inflationary procedure. Indeed, President Ford once estimated that creating a public-works job costs considerably more, on the average, than the work eventually performed is worth. In the end, the taxpayer pays, and that, too, adds to the force of inflation.

* * *

T. S. Eliot, the American-born poet who lived most of his adult life in Britain, once observed that "between the idea and the reality . . . falls the shadow." Many of the ideas put forward or supported by leaders of organized labor in the U.S. today appear, at first glance, to be beneficial to the country's economic health. A higher minimum wage will seemingly mean fatter paychecks all around. Tougher restraints on imported goods will seemingly protect jobs in "threatened" industries. More economic stimulation by Washington's policymakers will seemingly create more jobs, and, at the same time, reduce the unemployment rate.

However, as we have seen, such ideas, as excellent as they may initially sound, are not excellent at all. They are, in the main, detrimental—not only to the general health of the economy, but, particularly, to the American labor force, including its large contingent of union men and women.

Any lasting solution to America's economic dilemma necessitates dealing with the country's labor problem, just as it necessitates dealing with the problem of a ubiquitous governmental presence. And, clearly, the key to dealing with labor lies in dealing with the attitudes of a union leadership whose wrongheadness in the past does not inspire confidence that the leopard now will suddenly change its spots.

Yet, mistaken attitudes can be made to change. And one major reason for guarded optimism on this score is that a considerable amount of "shadow" has recently been falling across some venerable union ideas. First, there is the matter of pay. The recent woes of unionized construction workers were documented earlier in this chapter. Has the "reality" of their unemployment and their membership losses begun to prompt a more reasonable attitude on pay? There are a few indications that it has. In November 1977, for example, some 5,000 unionized bricklayers in New York City agreed to a 14.5 percent cut in wages and the elimination of various costly work rules involving overtime. "We recognize that the very survival of the skilled construction trades in our city is at stake," said Albert Cerussi, chairman of the union's New York District Council, at the time of the announcement. He hoped that the bricklayers' action might set a pattern for other unionized construction workers in the city. At the time, estimates placed the jobless rate among such workers at more than 50 percent. "The men need the work and the city needs the construction," Mr. Cerussi declared, adding that "our action should help to reduce costs and improve productivity."

Actual wage reductions remain the rare exception, rather than the rule. But there is evidence that pay increases among unionized construction workers generally have begun to moderate. For instance, the average annual pay boosts for construction-union journeymen during 1977 slowed to 6.3 percent, down from an average of about 10 percent only three years earlier.

Arnold Weber, dean of the Graduate School of Industrial Administration at Carnegie-Mellon University in Pittsburgh, believes that a more moderate approach to pay and a greater concern about productivity is not limited to unions in the building trades. "The persistence of high levels of unemployment has had a profound impact on all union leaders and members," he contends. "Their concern over job security would not be dissipated if unemployment dropped to 4 percent tomorrow."

An illustration of a more realistic attitude toward productivity can be found in a recent contract involving the International Association of Sheet Metal Workers. As an outgrowth of the contract, a training fund has been established, aimed at upgrading the skills and techniques of the union members involved in working on various new sorts of energy-generating facilities, such as solar plants. The training fund is jointly supported by the union and the managements of various companies in the energy business. The program covers 100,000 union journeymen and 10,000 apprentices and includes classroom instruction as well as on-the-job training.

Wilbur Fillippini, administrator of the program, maintains that it will provide contractors with "the highest skilled and best trained people, able to meet any competition" from nonunion workers who, he claims, "do not have the training facilities" available to their unionized counterparts.

* * *

A development that could hasten still more realistic attitudes among unions is the increasing involvement of organized labor in the executive suite. Such participation remains minimal in the U.S. But the practice has assumed considerable proportions in some countries abroad, particularly in West Germany, whose prosperity in recent years has been the envy of most industrial lands.

At present, union leaders in the U.S. demonstrate remarkably little concern about the profitability of the companies that provide them with jobs. On the contrary, much of the union rhetoric remains critical of alleged profit "windfalls" and corporate "ripoffs." However, if union members participated more fully in corporate affairs—in decision making and as shareowners—it seems probable that a greater productive effort would ensue. Certainly, the West German example suggests this. Under a so-called co-determination plan, worker representatives preside on corporate boards in West Germany. Powerful and financially secure West German unions "use their strength prudently because they know they have a stake in the economy and do not wish to endanger its growth," says Eileen B. Hoffman, a labor-relations specialist and the author of a Conference Board study of West German labor practices. It is not coincidental, she suggests, that Germany's rate of inflation, as well as its jobless rate, has consistently been lower than in nearly any other country, including the U.S. Moreover, she reports that "strikes are rare in Germany; 415 days per thousand wage and salary earners were lost because of strikes in the U.S. in 1975, only three days per thousand in Germany; in 1976, the U.S. figure was 487 days lost while in Germany, only 26."

Yet, she states, "German workers are among the most affluent in the world."

Is the German way exportable to the U.S.? Eileen Hoffman declares:

> Germans see worker representation on company boards as the way to democratize industry, to become social equals or partners, and to gain power. In America, liberals would demand inclusion of minorities, young people, and women on the boards to make these institutions more democratic and representative, to provide a communications link, and to influence policy decisions. . . . When American unions look at co-determination, they usually reject it outright because . . . it is felt that the adversary relationship and its fruits have preserved labor's equality and dignity vis-à-vis management.

Thomas R. Donahue, executive assistant to A.F.L-C.I.O. President George Meany, summed up the American labor-union position at an international conference on labor relations conducted in early 1977. "Because American unions have won equality at the bargaining table, we have not sought it in corporate boardrooms," Mr. Donahue stated. "We do not seek to be a partner in management. . . . We guard our independence fiercely—independent of government, independent of any political party and independent of management." The union official went on to declare:

> We have watched co-determination and its offshoot experiments with interest, and we will continue to do so, but it is our judgment that it offers little to American unions in the performance of their job unionism role . . . and it could only hurt U.S. unions as they pursue their social unionism functions, seeking legislation, political action, community involvement and a host of other approaches to improve the members' lot by improving society generally.

Machinists Union President William Winpinsinger has stated: "We have no acceptance in the American scene of unions being a coequal in the management of the industrial complex or even in terms of being political partners in the democratic process." And Mr. Donahue has argued: "We exist in a society hostile to trade unionism in a different way than is true in Europe. In our exclusive recognition-or-nothing system we go for broke against an employer who is fighting not against the way in which we work, not against the specifics we seek, but rather against our very existence in his plan."

Despite such commentary, there is reason to hope that long-standing attitudes may be changed in the U.S. Senator Jacob Javits, known as a friend of organized labor, maintains that he favors increased worker participation in the boardroom because "workers would not feel that profits had been taken out of their hides if they had a stake in them." Eileen Hoffman observes that "America has always been open to new ideas." As American trade unionists attend more conferences with their European counterparts, she adds, they will learn how some of the European ideas have worked out well.

* * *

Assuredly, there is nothing intrinsically lazy or inefficient about American working people. Quite the contrary. This truth was driven home to me several years ago. I spent a summer in London, attached to *The Wall Street Journal's* office there. From that office, I could see three beefy chaps apparently hired to repair the roof of a nearby building. Early in the summer, they had just begun to work on the roof. Three months later, when I got my last look at the trio, they were still at it, further along to be sure, but far short of finishing the job.

Their routine was simple: Arrive to work on the roof at about 10 A.M., have a chat, have tea (they had managed to rig an electrical outlet on the roof), chat some more, sit silently, perhaps hammer away at the roof briefly, disappear for lunch for a couple of hours, a bit more work, tea, chat and, around 4 P.M., disappear.

Christopher Lewinton, at the time serving as the managing director of Wilkinson Sword, the British razor-blade maker, explained during a London interview why he feels that British workers' tend to be less industrious than their American counterparts. He had spent much of his career in the U.S. as chief of Wilkinson's American operations. "You Americans don't have to cope with the problems of the class system, as we British employers do," he said. He explained that a new employee in a British company often comes to work with the attitude that there are very strict limits to how high he can ever rise within the firm because of his social background. "In the States," the executive added, "even the lowliest office clerk often has the idea, rightly or wrongly, that he can some day reach a much higher job level. As a result, he is generally willing to work harder than his British counterpart."

During my first week back in New York after the London assignment, I witnessed an enlightening contrast with the London rooftop scene. It was provided by three workmen who by coincidence happened to be repairing the roof at 15 East 74th Street in Manhattan, a few doors from my apartment. The job before them, I could see from my window, was strikingly similar to the job I had watched for so long in London. This time, however, the repair was completed in one week, and done well as far as my inexpert eye could determine.

I wondered whether the London crew had finished yet.

CHAPTER TWELVE

Directions to Go

There are many ways to explore the dilemma confronting America's economy. The unemployment-inflation bind, we have seen, is pervasive and multifaceted. Assuredly, it is not a matter that can be fully defined, much less resolved, through simply poring over a few key economic statistics. It is a matter fraught with imponderables and exceedingly difficult to resolve with wisdom.

Some directions, however, seem unmistakably appropriate. The need to reduce an increasingly pervasive, often suffocating governmental presence was noted in Chapter Ten. The need to deal with troubling aspects of American labor was discussed in Chapter Eleven. However, if the dilemma is ever to be resolved, additional moves appear essential.

A remarkable essay, written in 1977 by David P. Eastburn, president of the Philadelphia Federal Reserve Bank, assesses today's economic dilemma with clarity and precision. In the process, the Federal Reserve official indicates paths that seem likely, if followed, to bring a resolution much closer. Mr. Eastburn approaches the dilemma in fundamental terms. He sees it against a background of essential conflict, between what he terms Economic Man and Social Man. He differentiates between the two. Economic man, he explains, has particular concerns—production, quantity, goods and services, money values, work and discipline, competition, laissez-faire, inflation. Social Man, he writes, has other concerns, parallel but different—distribution, quality, people, human values, self-realization, cooperation, involvement, unemployment.

"It is easy," Mr. Eastburn concedes, "to overdraw the contrast between economic and social values." But he does offer this "shorthand list," as he calls it, of what seems "a kind of national schizophrenia which is both divisive and debilitating." In essence, he says, it is "the conflict between Economic Man and Social Man." When you read "quantity" for Economic Man, read "quality" for Social Man. When you read "work and discipline" for Economic Man, read "self-realization" for Social Man. When you read "laissez-faire" for Economic Man, read "involvement" for Social Man. And, at the bottom line, "inflation" for Economic Man becomes "unemployment" for Social Man.

"Economic Man is on one side," Mr. Eastburn says. "He has been telling the authorities—hang on; don't let up on efforts to curb inflation until you really have it licked; if this means recession, better pay the price now than a bigger one later."

On the "other side," says the Federal Reserve official, is "Social Man—he fears that a recession will hurt most those who are already disadvantaged; when unemployment rises, as it must when the economy slows, those who are laid off first are the unskilled; efforts to recruit workers from the ghetto are suspended; Social Man, therefore, is inclined to trade inflation for jobs."

In a sense, Mr. Eastburn personalizes the economy's dilemma. He confesses that "it is not exactly clear why these positions are held as firmly as they are." He stresses that, quite clearly, "there are economic and social costs in both inflation and recession." Both, he knows, "can destroy our economy." And, he warns, this entire matter is "an issue of great significance to the entire economy" which, he adds, has tended "to become polarized."

* * *

In Mr. Eastburn's view, to resolve the unemployment-inflation dilemma facing the American economy is to resolve the conflict between Economic Man and Social Man. Any resolution, he believes, will be painful. But not impossible. Compromise and patience are essential. "Social Man's best hope is to work with Economic Man toward the kind of dynamic economy that will make . . . a happy solution," he says. "Social problems cannot be solved without a strong and growing economy, and we cannot prosper economically if we continue to have large parts of the population not sharing in the fruits of production."

Mr. Eastburn clearly takes an optimistic view. He sees that compromise and patience will be required. But he also believes that they will be practiced. Economic Man, he feels, "is most adaptable. He is not the same person now as 50 or 75 years ago. The rough edges of his philosophy and practice have been smoothed by social action—especially in the 1930's." Moreover, the bank official continues, Economic Man "will not be the same person in 25 years as now. But he will still have an important role to play in our society." At the same time, Mr. Eastburn is convinced that Social Man can come to understand the "economic lesson," that limited resources "force us to make hard decisions about priorities."

The tradeoff is "tough," as the official puts it. The task will be "to heed the urgings from the heart of Social Man and, at the same time, the advice from the head of Economic Man."

The question of unemployment illustrates the difficulty involved. "Social Man is inclined to accept some inflation to get lower unemployment," Mr. Eastburn states, while "Economic Man would accept some unemployment to hold down inflation." On this key issue, he confides that he feels "more comfortable with the view of Economic Man; there are limits to how far we can push the economy without setting off skyrocketing inflation." The Fed official declares that "I, for one, want to proceed very carefully about forcing unemployment down" through any highly stimulative economic measures. There are, he stresses, additional ways to tackle the problem.

One direction that seems promising involves a degree of compromise. Economic Man abhors, for example, any solution that would rely upon the concept of a wholly regimented economy, directed by the Washington bureaucracy. Social Man abhors, in contrast, the idea that a wholly unfettered marketplace, entirely free of governmental direction, would resolve the economy's dilemma. However, a broad range of action—involving careful structural innovations—is possible between the two extremes of total regimentation and total freedom. Mr. Eastburn, among others, sees a great potential within this area. Broad economic measures simply "can't do the whole job" of concurrently curbing inflation and trimming joblessness, he says. "Structural measures" are required.

* * *

Arthur Burns, the former Federal Reserve Board chairman, agrees. To a disturbing extent, he says, the unemployment-inflation dilemma "has its roots in the structure of our economic institutions." He maintains that new structural initiatives seem essential, for example, in the area of job training. We saw earlier that the country's educational system has tended in recent years to generate a great many individuals who are highly trained in skills where general demand is unfortunately very low. A problem is evident as well at less highly trained educational levels where the governmental hand has been at work. In a recent 12-year span, nearly 12 million persons enrolled in federal manpower-training projects, ranging from the Neighborhood Youth Corps to the Job Corps. The federal expense involved exceeded $14 billion. This is no inconsiderable amount, even in this inflationary era. Yet, the various federal job-training efforts clearly failed to produce the sort of full employment that advocates of such programs had envisaged. An additional job-training effort was launched in 1973, with the passage of the Comprehensive Employment and Training Act. This legislation, known as CETA, places the responsibility for planning and implementing job training at state and local governmental levels instead of in Washington's hands. CETA means the pouring of many more millions of taxpayer funds into job training. Perhaps such efforts will eventually begin to generate young workers appropriately trained to fill many of the thousands of jobs that, as we have seen, go begging no matter how high the overall unemployment rate may be.

A first step, we submit, would be to scrutinize more carefully how effectively such job-training endeavors may be faring. "There is a desperate need for more research in this area to try to identify which, if any, elements of training programs have been successful," says Mr. Eastburn of the Philadelphia Fed. He adds: "We are still a long way from understanding the relation between manpower training and employment experience, but what limited evidence exists generally shows that government training programs have positive, but rather small, economic effects."

An illustration of the need for more detail can be found in the announcement of a new federal effort to provide work for unemployed teen-agers residing within a half dozen inner-city neighborhoods marked by especially widespread unemployment. Under the program, announced by the Labor Department in early 1978, the six areas would receive federal grants of more than $15 million each to initiate programs guaranteeing jobs to all teen-agers in the respective neighborhoods who want work and, at the same time, are willing to remain in school. Under the plan, any person 16 through 19 years old who comes from a low-income family is promised up to 20 hours a week of work during the school year and 40 hours weekly in the summer. To obtain a job, the youths need only apply. The pay, according to the announcement, is at the minimum wage or slightly above it.

The plan is doubtless laudable in many respects. Certainly, inner-city teen-agers constitute a particularly distressing aspect of the broad problem of unemployment. But all sorts of nagging questions are left hanging. How is "low-income" defined? What sort of work is to be offered? What training will be imparted that could lead to long-term employment? How will the youths involved be taught to understand the importance of job-discipline when, according to the announcement, the jobs are "guaranteed"? If the pay rates exceed the minimum wage, as the plan indicates may be the situation, how will other workers in jobs paying only the minimum wage react? How will the youths themselves ever be willing to seek employment elsewhere that might be available and more enduring, but only pays the minimum wage? Who will administer the six programs? Will the cost of the jobs to taxpayers exceed the value of the services rendered by the participating youths?

A beginning toward any successful job-training program for the young, we submit, is to ascertain fields where the enduring openings are most likely to materialize. Studies have been undertaken for this purpose. More attention should be paid to the findings than, we suspect, is the case. One that deserves close attention from governmental planners is a 1976 analysis by the Conference Board. Among the findings is that about 1.8 million jobs are likely to open up by 1985. Of these, the largest single group of openings is expected to be in the clerical field, where 795,000 openings are projected. The next largest group of openings is expected to be in skilled services, with 429,000 new jobs foreseen; these would include health-care workers, security personnel, food-service workers, hairdressers and other such occupations. In all, 123 fields of endeavor are expected to provide employment opportunities. By and large, the study states, they are jobs that "do not require a college degree." At the same time, however, the report makes clear that the country's vocational-training facilities may prove inadequate to the task of filling all the projected openings. And certainly, such programs as the aforementioned make-work plan for teenagers in the six inner-city neighborhoods hold little promise of equipping the participants to become, say, competent filing clerks or health-care workers.

* * *

There is no good reason why vocational training in the U.S. cannot play an important role in the battle to bring down joblessness with a minimum of inflationary pressure. Such training has long been useful in helping other countries to keep joblessness at a minimal level. Indeed, a U.S. Labor Department study attributes relatively low teen-age unemployment in many nations abroad in part at least to the fact that "vocational guidance and apprenticeship play a major role in . . . absorbing teen-agers into the work force." In the U.S., in contrast, the study finds that "there is seldom anyone to advise young persons about what kinds of jobs exist, what employment they might like to try, or how to go about obtaining a job; young people are often left to their own devices in the employment search."

In West Germany, the report notes, "nearly all students receive comprehensive vocational orientation before graduation." In Britain, it continues, "staff members of the Youth Employment Service counsel nearly 80 percent of school-leavers who are not going to universities." In Sweden, the report adds, "vocational orientation begins in the sixth school year, and during the eighth year all children have an opportunity to work at a job of their choice for three weeks."

In the U.S., by comparison, officials estimate that fewer than half of high school graduates not entering college are in any sort of job-training program. Recently, only 379,000 youths were signed up in formal apprenticeship programs in the U.S. As noted in Chapter Three, there is apparently a connection between lower teen-age unemployment rates in key countries abroad and the fact that the countries involved generally do not have minimum-wage regulations applying to youths. The Labor Department study of job training in the U.S. and abroad also suggests that this may be a major factor in the relative success of foreigners in curbing unemployment among young people.

Other reports indicate that private companies abroad may be taking a more active role in seeing to it that teen-age unemployment gets high-priority attention. In Britain, such large companies as Imperial Chemical Industries, Rank Xerox, Rolls-Royce and Tate & Lyle have begun giving their top executives leaves of absence to provide them time to help in local community efforts aimed at finding jobs for young people. ICI recently increased hiring for its apprentice program by fifty percent. In Belgium, selected large corporations have agreed to insure that at least one percent of their work force is under the age of 24. It is not the sort of employment policy that would win warm-hearted support from the AFL-CIO. But it is the sort of policy that must be considered, in a spirit of compromise, if headway is to be made against joblessness among the American young.

* * *

Resolving the unemployment-inflation dilemma that besets America's economy must require a spirit of compromise, as well as much patience, on many fronts. The point was stressed earlier that a vibrant, growing economy will most surely prosper in an economic environment where marketplace forces are allowed to flourish. The "invisible hand" that Adam Smith admired, discussed in Chapter One, must be allowed to perform its beneficent functions.

It is not enough, however, simply to protect, for example, against the trap of central planning, whose dangers were documented in Chapter Nine. Resolving the economy's overriding problem necessitates a large additional step. As David Eastburn puts it, "Economic Man should be encouraged to do his thing." Doing it well, of course, requires a marketplace that is free and competitive. And it also requires, as the Federal Reserve official so correctly emphasizes, a reasonable degree of incentive. For example, he worries that the country's present, relatively generous unemployment insurance system probably reduces the incentive to work, which in turn tends to amplify unemployment and aggravate inflation. "I would lean toward some adjustments," he says, "such as taxing unemployment benefits." Any such steps would require a considerable amount of political courage, as well as a large degree of compromise on the part of Social Man.

A study by the Paris-based Organization for Economic Cooperation and Development shows that a relatively large portion of the American work force is indeed covered by unemployment benefits. The U.S. rate of 95 percent tops comparable rates of 80 percent in Britain, 93 percent in West Germany, 61 percent in France, 51 percent in Italy and only 45 percent in Japan. A study by the economics department of Morgan Guaranty Trust of New York also indicates that America's unemployment insurance system is relatively generous. The amount of jobless benefits in most key countries, including the U.S., comes to slightly more than half of average weekly pay. However, the bank's analysis shows that the maximum duration of such benefits tends to be exceptionally long in the U.S. The average U.S. duration of 65 weeks, according to Morgan Guaranty at the time of its study, compares with 50 weeks in Japan, 52 weeks in West Germany and Britain and 26 weeks in Italy.

"The major question is whether or not unemployment compensation discourages work effort and prolongs unemployment," the study declares. The report indicates that this may indeed be the situation, stating that "a hard look at the entire program is long overdue" in the U.S. The bank cautions that "a key misconception is that jobless pay is a pittance, only a small fraction of what was received by the worker on the job; actually, when allowance is made for the fact that jobless pay is tax-free, benefits replace, on a conservative basis, two-thirds or more of previous net income." In fact, the report finds that "in some states, which also pay a dependent's allowance to the unemployed, income for not working can exceed after-tax income when on the job."

Quite clearly, the U.S. system of providing generous payments to tide workers over periods of joblessness contains a variety of highly desirable features. The benefits tend, for example, to prevent periods of economic recession from becoming too severe by shoring up consumer buying power. The deep economic depression of the 1930's would likely have been less severe if anything approaching the current arrangement had been in force then. In strictly humanitarian terms, it is impossible to argue against a reasonably generous benefit program.

Yet, as the Morgan Guaranty report suggests, such benefits, in the U.S. especially, have swelled to a point where they may indeed discourage "work effort"—which in turn discourages productivity and aggravates inflation and may also prolong unemployment. There is evidence, as well, that the program has encouraged what amounts to widespread cheating by individuals. A survey by *The New York Times,* for instance, finds "widespread abuses of a system that was originally designed as a short-term bridge to help people between jobs." The survey, moreover, finds that the abuses "have arisen largely because the aid programs have expanded so rapidly that officials [in charge] have not been able to police them properly." One administrator says that "we found that we were too busy writing checks to enforce even the most basic regulations." He estimates that "about 15 percent of those getting a weekly check were abusers." Examples cited range from a Los Angeles construction worker drawing $104 weekly in unemployment benefits while building his own house and regularly turning down jobs to work at his trade to the wife of a $35,000-a-year New York City executive who managed through a friend to have her job eliminated so that she could become eligible to draw about $100 a week for doing nothing.

The Carter Administration, fortunately, is beginning to test just how willing the unemployed are to look for jobs. Under a law which the President signed in April 1977, federal supplemental unemployment benefits are now denied to anyone who fails to accept any offer of suitable work or to apply for any suitable work to which the individual is referred. The law also cuts back slightly the maximum duration of federal jobless benefits. Such regulations may not please Mr. Eastburn's Social Man. But the law does typify precisely the sort of structural steps that must be taken if American leaders are to tackle with any success the country's economic dilemma. It marks a beginning, hopefully, of a political awareness in Washington—in the White House and the Congress—that restoring the incentive to work is a consideration that must not be overlooked.

A somewhat similar situation prevails all across the broad welfare front. The massive governmental sums devoted to various welfare programs were discussed earlier. The inflationary ramifications of such federal largess have been indicated with considerable dismay. On a more encouraging note, however, it is significant that here and there evidence is beginning to appear of a new willingness to correct welfare abuses and, at the same time, inject a modicum of frugality into some of these programs.

New York City's massive welfare rolls, for example, have been declining for a number of years. Officials there attribute the drop, pronounced since mid-1976, to a tightening of approval procedures for applicants. In mid-1977, 48 percent of all new welfare applicants in the city were turned down, compared with a rejection rate of only 25 percent several years earlier. In early 1978, some 934,000 New Yorkers were receiving some form of welfare assistance. This was down from 1,077,000 five years earlier. One weapon in the battle to trim the city's welfare rolls has been the computer. A computer-based program, for example, now matches the names of welfare recipients against Social Security files to see who may have received aid while failing to report being employed. Another computer match-up checks for automobile license records of would-be welfare recipients. A recipient now is not permitted to own a car unless he can prove that it is essential to his employment. Such efforts have led to a reduction in the rolls of nearly 13,000 persons in a single month.

The paring of New York's welfare rolls, it should be added, has not led to an actual reduction in welfare expenses in the city. This is because individual relief payments have continued to be expanded in order to compensate for the rising overall cost of living. However, without the new toughness regarding applications, the city's welfare costs would have risen far more sharply than has recently been the case.

* * *

All attempts to improve the economy's general health by inducing a greater sense of work incentive would doubtless fail without concurrent efforts, on a broader scale, to strengthen the entire competitive system. Directions toward this end have been suggested by Arthur Burns, among other economists. In an address at the University of Georgia in the fall of 1975, the former Federal Reserve Board chairman put forward proposals aimed at pumping new competitive vigor into the U.S. economy. He suggested, for example, that a hard new look be taken at a variety of inflationary programs tending to sap "competitive enterprise" in the U.S. He mentioned, particularly, import quotas, trade tariffs and price-maintenance laws. "If we are to have any chance of ridding our economy of its inflationary bias," he declared, "we must at least be willing to reopen our economic minds." He stressed first, the crucial economic role of productivity. And he urged "overhauling the structure of federal taxation, so as to increase incentives for business capital spending" to make the country's factories more efficient and its workers more productive. Along the same line, he warned against overzealous efforts by bureaucrats to impose "environmental and safety regulations." He urged "stretching out the timetables for achieving our environmental and safety goals." Otherwise, he feared "the dampening effect of excessive governmental regulations on business activity."

A particularly worrisome omen for U.S. productivity, deemed so important by Mr. Burns, shows up in data on investment in research and development. The country's annual rate of growth in R&D spending, after eliminating increases due simply to rising prices, has been dropping gradually since the early 1950's. Then, the annual rate of R&D increase amounted to more than nine percent. A decade later, the rate of growth had dropped to less than five percent annually. By the late 1960's, it was below the two percent mark.

And since then, it has been nearly flat from year to year. Moreover, more of the R&D total has tended of late to be directed into military purposes, an area where spending, as we have seen, is apt to generate inflationary pressures. It is no coincidence that a parallel slowdown in U.S. patents is evident. Or that the ratio of scientists and engineers to the total population has declined in the U.S. in recent years. In most other major industrial countries, in contrast, this important ratio has continued to climb. All this is distressing because R&D spending tends to create jobs through the eventual introduction of new and better products. Studies show, moreover, that high growth rates in R&D spending and sharp advances in worker productivity go hand in hand. The reason is that technological breakthroughs in production procedure are likelier when R&D outlays are substantial.

In his Georgia talk, Mr. Burns also urged that "a vigorous search should be made for ways to enhance price competition among our nation's business enterprises." The country must find the courage, he said, "to reassess laws directed against restraint of trade by business firms and to improve the enforcement of these laws."

On this score, happily, there appears to be a wide consensus among policymakers. On any political spectrum, Mr. Burns ranks considerably to the right of the economic staff of the Joint Economic Committee of the Congress, which the late Senator Humphrey once chaired. Yet, in 1976, the JEC released a study suggesting that the Justice Department's antitrust division "may not be using its enforcement resources to their best advantage." In effect, the JEC report urged a tougher federal effort to prevent and "to punish price-fixing conspiracies and to forestall mergers that threaten competition." It is a point of view that Arthur Burns clearly also endorses.

While tougher antitrust enforcement would most likely benefit the U.S. economy in the long run, there can be little question that an easing of the country's tax burden would also prove beneficial. One indication that the national tax burden needs to be eased can be found in a 1977 study by Peter Gutmann, chairman of the department of economics and finance at City University of New York. He estimates that a "subterranean economy" exists in America whose gross national product—conservatively—approximates $176 billion. This sum, the CUNY professor adds, amounts to nearly 10 percent of the country's money supply. This "subterranean economy" is lubricated, Mr. Gutmann says, "by currency in circulation outside banks," a supply of funds amounting to some $361 per capita, or $1,523 per family of four.

This "subterranean economy" does not show up in the familiar yardsticks, such as the gross national product, by which the Washington statistic mills delineate the overall economy's dimensions. Mr. Gutmann reckons, for example, that the subterranean economy provides jobs for more than eight million Americans. They work for cash, because this tactic allows them to accumulate income outside the tax collector's purview. They include the retired, drawing Social Security, illegal aliens and other such individuals. "Like black markets throughout the world," Mr. Gutmann says, "the subterranean economy was created by government rules and restrictions." It is, he says, "a creature of income and other taxes; we should recognize it is created by government and admit that increasing public contempt for the tax system and government regulation is causing it to grow more rapidly than ever."

The professor urges a course of action. "We must take a long, hard look at the rules, regulations, restrictions and taxes that have spawned the subterranean economy," he declares. "If we fail to do so, an ever larger part of the total economy will go underground." The economist spells out one way in which such a development could greatly aggravate inflationary pressure in the country. Jobholders within the subterranean economy do not show up in the official employment figures that authorities in Washington review when they set economic policy. As a consequence, there is a tendency to believe that considerably more slack exists in the country's labor reserve than is actually the case. This, in turn, may lead to overly stimulative, inflation-producing economic measures. In addition, of course, since no tax revenues are collected within the subterranean economy, governmental budget deficits, which also are inflationary, tend to be larger than would otherwise be the case.

A small first step in the direction of easing the tax burden is simply to reduce the various tax rates, up and down the line, for corporations as well as for individuals. A secondary measure, so long as inflation keeps propelling taxpayers into higher and higher tax brackets, would be to index the country's tax system. Under this arrangement, in brief outline, a taxpayer pushed into a higher tax bracket by a pay increase would not shell out a larger percentage of his income unless the raise in pay exceeded the increase in living costs. About at dozen countries index income taxes to some extent. Their experience indicates that the idea is both practical from a bureaucratic standpoint and an effective means of easing the load on taxpayers.

* * *

Perhaps the importance of more governmental concern about restoring individual incentive can best be driven home by a horrendous example of how individual incentive is occasionally suppressed, even stamped out, by the bureaucracy.

A federal judge in Rochester, N.Y., in 1977 ruled against a husband and wife there, a Mr. and Mrs. Paul Brennan. The Brennans had been operating the P. H. Brennan Hand Delivery Service since March 1976, after the United States Postal Service stirred Mrs. Brennan's anger by taking two weeks to deliver a letter from a friend of hers in Idaho. The Brennans' service guaranteed same-day delivery of letters within the city's business district, for 10 cents apiece, or three cents under the Postal Service charge. The Postal Service brought a civil action against the Brennans, alleging that their enterprise violated statutes that grant the Postal Service a monopoly over the delivery of first-class mail. The Brennans, in their defense, contended that the statutes are unconstitutional on the ground that they exceed the power of the government to deal with the nation's mail.

The couple is planning to appeal the District Court's decision. Whether they ultimately win or not, however, their predicament illustrates in harsh terms the difficulty that citizens with even an exceptional degree of initiative can encounter. It is precisely the sort of predicament that should not be allowed to develop if Uncle Sam is ever to put his economic house back in order. As Governor Edmund Brown of California has observed: "We're making it more difficult for people to go out and undertake their own enterprise," and this in turn "is really weakening the spirit of this country."

There are countless ways, of course, by which individual incentive can be encouraged. In the case of the Brennans, for instance, a hard look at statutes covering first-class mail is clearly in order. Whatever the means, however, the end is the same—to revitalize an economy plagued by the twin evils of unemployment and inflation.

* * *

The dilemma of joblessness and rapidly climbing prices will not be resolved quickly. Nor will it be resolved simply. We have seen that a wide-ranging effort is required. The problem must be put into perspective. For instance, we have seen that inflation is perhaps a nastier matter than is generally supposed, and that the unemployment rate may provide an overly dismal picture of what is actually transpiring on the labor front. We have reviewed the broad forces that perpetuate the price spiral, from excessive generation of money at the Federal Reserve Board to spendthrift attitudes in the Congress and at the White House. In an address at Yale University in June 1962, President John F. Kennedy declared that "the myth persists that federal deficits create inflation." The economic record during much of the period since that address makes clear that what Mr. Kennedy believed to be a myth was in fact the truth.

We have seen that a healthy economy will require more than simply more judicious monetary and fiscal policies in Washington. There are, we have seen, traps waiting on the road ahead that must be avoided. There is the difficult business of coping somehow with much unnecessary and harmful governmental regulation. Happily, in his 1978 State of the Union Address, President Carter displayed a keen awareness of this problem. There is also the difficult matter of dealing with a labor leadership which, whatever its virtues, seems wrongheaded in its approach to key economic matters.

All told, the directions that must be followed, if the country is to emerge from its economic bind, are many. But they are directions that can be followed. It is feasible, for instance, to roll back governmental regulations and yet fully understand that the government, in the twentieth century in America, must remain a significant presence at federal, state and local levels. The economy will necessarily remain mixed—a governmental side and private enterprise.

Indeed, a mixed economy in no way precludes a vastly healthier economic climate than now exists. "I believe we can have a mixed economy that works," asserts Gabriel Hauge, chairman of Manufacturers Hanover Trust in New York. "The key is an environment that is congenial to the entrepreneurial spirit." The bank official ticks off a list of suggestions. They include a renewed recognition "that the dynamism of our country derives from the work-risk-reward ethic of the market system." He advocates as well "rifle-shot techniques instead of shotgun-demand increases to reduce structural unemployment." He also would encourage more research-and-development projects and, at the ballot box, reject political "candidates who seek today's votes with tomorrow's debts."

Mr. Hauge is not alone in his optimistic view that a healthier economy is possible. Another optimist is Bruce C. Netschert, a private economist who has taught at Cornell University and the University of Minnesota. Mr. Netschert approaches the country's economic dilemma with additional expertise—he is also a trained geologist. His optimism relates to a special aspect of the economic dilemma—the much-publicized idea that U.S. economic progress in the years just ahead will be severely hampered by dire shortages of major raw materials. Such shortages, of course, would tend to cause unemployment and aggravate inflation. However, Mr. Netschert is convinced that "no true scarcity situation will develop" during coming decades for the United States. There are, he stresses, "abundant low-grade resources of the major structural metals, such as iron and aluminum." He cites, in addition, "the inexhaustable quantity of ordinary igneous rock containing concentrations of many needed materials and deep-sea mining of the marine environment." He also notes that the substitution of manmade products should continue to prevent scarcity problems from arising.

Even if Mr. Netschert's optimism proves excessive, this would not weaken the argument for endeavoring to restore competitive forces within the economy. As David Eastburn explains, a finite supply of industrial resources only increases the importance of having a freely competitive marketplace. "The market system, if it is permitted to work, can slow down use of increasingly scarce resources and encourage development of new resources," he says. He explains, for instance, that if the price of gasoline is permitted to rise freely, according to demand, this will cut down demand and also encourage exploration for new energy sources. "The trick," he says, "is for government to work as much as possible through the market system and to capitalize on Economic Man's desire for profits and his talent in allocating resources."

Perhaps, in the end, the greatest danger to America's economic future is the possibility that Americans will begin to accept the notion that the present dilemma cannot be resolved, that the country must live indefinitely with a high degree of both unemployment and inflation. This need not be. It will not be if enough citizens, starting with the President in the White House, move in directions that may not always be easy but ultimately will bring about a far healthier economy than that which currently exists in America.

Index

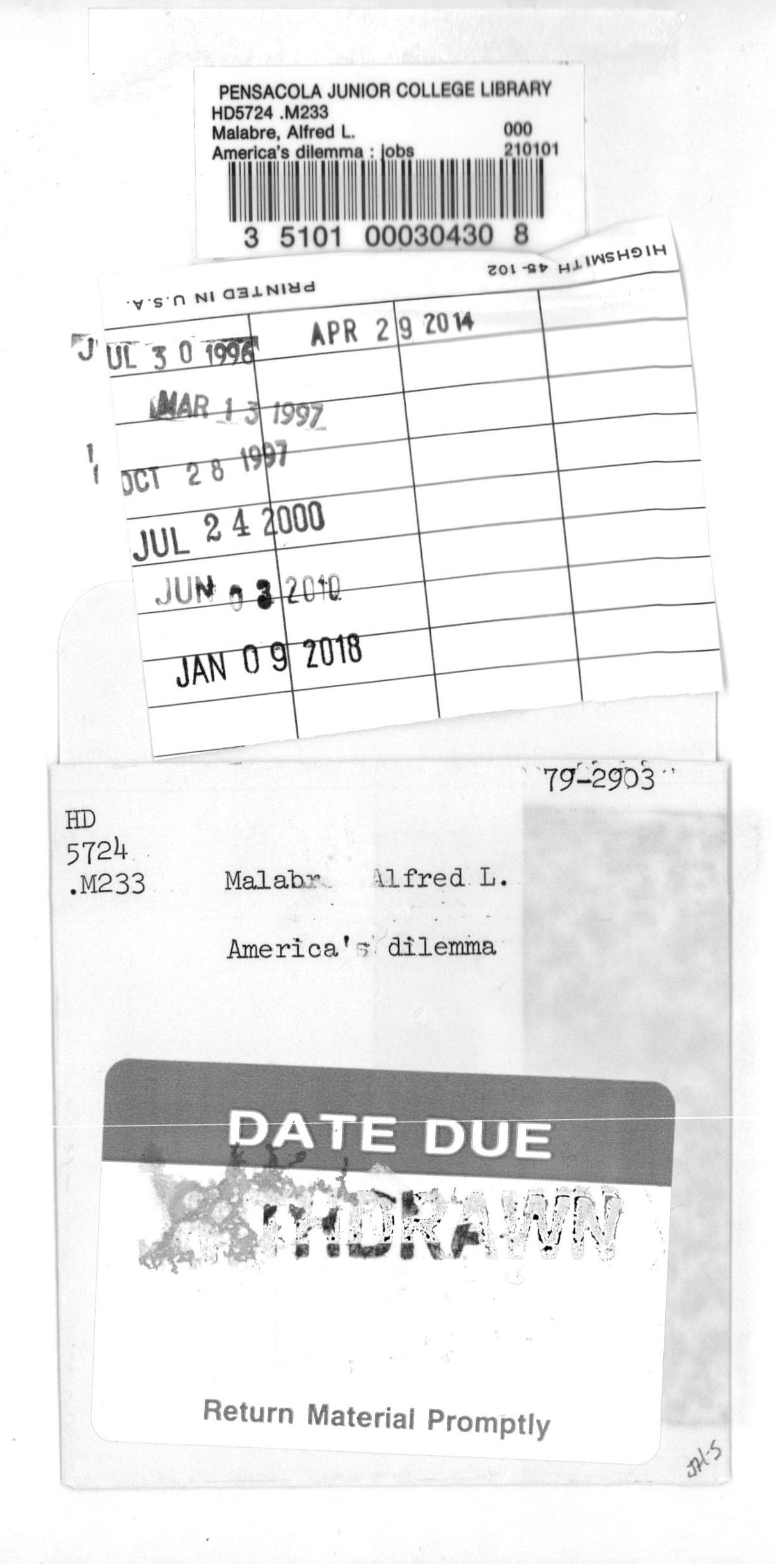

PENSACOLA JUNIOR COLLEGE LIBRARY
HD5724 .M233
Malabre, Alfred L.
000
America's dilemma : jobs
210101
3 5101 00030430 8
HIGHSMITH 45-102
PRINTED IN U.S.A.
JUL 3 0 1996
APR 2 9 2014
MAR 1 3 1997
OCT 2 8 1997
JUL 2 4 2000
JUN 0 3 2010
JAN 0 9 2018
79-2903
HD
5724
.M233
Malabre, Alfred L.
America's dilemma
DATE DUE
WITHDRAWN
Return Material Promptly